LORDSHIP

Karyn Henley

Standard
PUBLISHING
CINCINNATI, OHIO

LORDSHIP
The foundation for following God

FOUNDATIONS CURRICULUM®

Published by Standard Publishing, Cincinnati, Ohio
A division of Standex International Corporation

Credits
Cover design by Brian Fowler
Interior design by Jeff Richardson
Cover and inside illustrations by Ed Koehler
Project editors: Ruth Frederick, Bruce E. Stoker

09 08 07 06 05 04 03   6 5 4 3 2
ISBN 0-7847-1366-9
Printed in the United States of America

TABLE OF CONTENTS

Table of Contents
Table of Contents

INTRODUCTION

The Irish poet William Butler Yeats once said, "Education is not the filling of a pail, but the lighting of a fire." In the first temple, the tent of meeting, there was a lampstand. God's instructions were, "Tell the people of Israel to bring you pure olive oil for the lampstand, so it can be kept burning continually. . . . Aaron and his sons will keep the lamps burning in the Lord's presence day and night" (Exodus 27:20, 21, NLT). Today we are God's temple (1 Corinthians 3:16). And our passion, our living love for the Lord, keeps our lampstand burning before him. (See Revelation 2:4, 5.) Our job in the spiritual education of children is to light a fire, a living, growing love for God within them.

The Foundations curriculum can help light that fire. Each of our students is a temple of God. So the goal of the Foundations curriculum is to construct within children the essential foundations upon which they can build (and sustain) a loving, thriving relationship with the Lord. To do this, the Foundations curriculum provides a thorough, step-by-step, in-depth exploration of the following foundations.

Quarter 1: Studying the Bible, The Foundation for Knowing God

Quarter 2: Salvation, The Foundation for Living with God

Quarter 3: Prayer, The Foundation for Growing Closer to God

Quarter 4: Worship, The Foundation for Loving God

Quarter 5: Lordship, The Foundation for Following God

Quarter 6: Stewardship, The Foundation for Reflecting God

Quarter 7: Missions, The Foundation for Sharing God

Quarter 8: Making Peace, The Foundation for Living in Fellowship

This curriculum is intended for use with students in third through fifth grades. Each quarter is independent of the others, so they can be taught in any order. In fact, each quarter can be used as a single unit to fill in a 13-week study at any time of the year and can be followed or preceded by any other curriculum of your choice.

The following arrangement is a suggestion showing how the Foundations Curriculum can be taught in two years. Studying the Bible (September-November), Salvation (December-February), Prayer (March-May), Worship (June-August), Lordship (September-November), Stewardship (December-February), Missions (March-May), Making Peace (June-August).

WALK THROUGH A WEEK

SCRIPTURE AND GOAL

The session begins with a Scripture and a simple goal. You may use the Scripture as a memory verse if you wish, or you may use it to support the theme for the day, reading the Scripture when you gather for the first prayer.

INTRODUCTORY ACTIVITY

You can begin your introductory activity as soon as the first student arrives, guiding others to join you as they come into your room. This activity serves two purposes. First, it gives the students something fun to do from the first moment they arrive. Second, it starts thoughts and conversations about the theme of the session. Talking is encouraged. Questions are welcome. Get to know your students. Make it your goal to discover something interesting and special about each one. Let them know that their mission is to discover more about God and about how they can get to know him better every day, so that God becomes their constant companion, their treasured friend, their awesome king.

DISCOVERY RALLY

Gather the students together as a group in preparation for the Discovery centers.

What's the Good Word? This is a time to read the Scripture for the day. You may also sing a few songs if you want.

Challenge. This is a time to introduce the students to the theme for the day by making challenging statements or asking challenging questions.

Prayer. Choose a student to lead a prayer of blessing for the day's activities, asking God to open your hearts and teach everyone present.

DISCOVERY CENTERS

You will need either one teacher/facilitator for each center, or clearly written instructions that tell the students what they are to do in the center.

The way your class uses Discovery Centers will depend on how much time you have and how many students there are in your class.

- If you have a few students, go together to as many centers as you can in the time you have.
- If you have more than ten students and lots of time, divide into three groups. Send

one group to each center and let each group rotate to a different center as they finish the activity, so that each student gets to go to each center during Discovery Center time.

• If you have more than ten students, but little time, divide into groups of three. Number off, one to three in each group. Each student #1 goes to the first center, #2 goes to the second, #3 goes to the third. After each center has completed its activity, the original groups of three come back together again to tell each other what they learned in their centers.

• Or you may choose to let all three centers do the same activity. Choose the one or two activities that you think your students will enjoy most. Divide the students into groups for centers, and once they are there, do not rotate. Instead, let each group do the one or two activities you have chosen.

DEBRIEFING QUESTIONS

If you have time, gather together as a large group at the end of the session to ask and answer questions and discuss the theme and/or other issues on the students' minds.

Review the Scripture for the day.

PRAY

You or a student may close your class time in prayer.

SUGGESTED BIBLE STUDY HELPS

This is by no means a complete list. As you look for these, you will find others that may be just as interesting and helpful.

Bible Handbooks

What the Bible Is All About, Henrietta C. Mears (Gospel Light)

What the Bible Is All About for Young Explorers, Frances Blankenbaker (Gospel Light)

The International Children's Bible Handbook, Lawrence Richards (Word)

The Baker Bible Handbook for Kids, Marek Lugowski and Carol J. Smith (Baker)

New Unger's Bible Handbook: Student Edition, Merrill Unger (Moody)

Bible Encyclopedias

The Children's Bible Encyclopedia: The Bible Made Simple and Fun, Mark Water (Baker Books)

Bible Dictionaries

International Children's Bible Dictionary, Lynn Waller (Word)

The Baker Bible Dictionary for Kids (Baker)

Bible Fact Books

The Awesome Book of Bible Facts, Sandy Silverthorne (Harvest House)

The Baker Book of Bible People for Kids (Baker)

The Complete Book of Bible Trivia, J. Stephen Lang (Tyndale)

For Teachers and Older Students

Willmington's Bible Handbook, Harold L. Willmington (Tyndale)

Holman Topical Concordance (Holman Bible Publishers)

Holman Bible Dictionary (Holman Bible Publishers)

Children's Ministry Resource Edition (Thomas Nelson)

Manners and Customs in the Bible, Victor H. Matthews (Hendrickson)

What Does "Lord" Mean?

Scripture

"The God who made the world and everything in it is the Lord of heaven and earth."   Acts 17:24, NIV

Goal

Learn that "Lord" means ruler or authority.

INTRODUCTION

Make two copies of the Insignias sheet (page 14). From one copy, cut out the insignias so that there is one insignia for each student. Display the other copy in the room. As students enter, give each one an insignia and ask them to find out whether they are in the army or navy. Then they should find out what rank they are and who is above them in rank and below them in rank. If you have time, ask them to sit two groups, army and navy, according to their rank. (Note: These are insignias for the U.S. Army and Navy. If you are using this in another country, use that country's insignias if possible.)

DISCOVERY RALLY

Discovery Rally Discovery Rally Rally

Gather the students together in a large group.

WHAT'S THE GOOD WORD?

Choose a student to read the Scripture for the day.

THE CHALLENGE

Choose one or two children from each group (army and navy) to tell what their rank is and who is above them and below them in rank. Ask: **What is the rank of the person who is highest in command in each group?** Start with the student holding the lowest rank, and ask: **Who gets to tell you what to do?** Do this with several students. Ask: **Do you have to do what you're told to do? Why? Why do armies, navies, and other groups of armed forces have leaders with the authority to order people around? Do you think these leaders ever make mistakes in ordering their people to do something? Why?**

Tell the students that during the next few weeks, you will be discovering more about the greatest leader of all, the One who is in charge of heaven and earth, the Lord of all. Tell them that in their Discovery Centers today they will find out what "Lord" really means.

PRAYER

DISCOVERY CENTERS

Discovery Cen Discovery Center

1. BANNERS

DO: Turn the cards face down and spread them out on the table. Ask each student to choose a card and look up the Scripture. Then give each student a rectangle of felt. Ask them to fold the piece of felt in half lengthwise. Then they should

MATERIALS

Bibles, one 9" x 11 1/4" piece of felt of any color for each student, rulers, scissors, pens, puffy or glittery fabric paint, 15 index cards with one Scripture reference written on each: Genesis 14:22; Nehemiah 1:5; Jeremiah 23:6; Hebrews 13:20; Matthew 9:38; Matthew 11:25; Matthew 12:8; 2 Thessalonians 3:16; Matthew 20:30; Luke 2:11; John 13:14; Acts 4:33; Acts 11:17; Revelation 19:16.

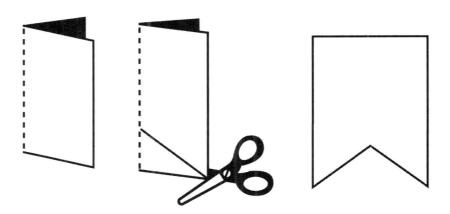

measure three inches along the fold and make a dot. Next they draw a diagonal line from the dot to each the closest corner as shown and cut along that line through both layers of felt. They open the larger felt piece. On this banner, they use the puffy or glittery fabric paint to write the name of the Lord that they discovered in their Scripture.

DISCUSS: As the students work on their banners, ask them if they know what "Lord" means. After some discussion, ask the students who read an Old Testament Scripture to tell if they saw anything unusual about the word "Lord" in their Scriptures. "Lord" was probably written in all capital letters. That means that the word stands for God's name, YHWH, which in English is "Jehovah." In other Scriptures we find the word "Lord" in lower-case letters. Then it means ruler or authority, the one in charge. Say: **Just because people call Jesus "Lord" doesn't necessarily mean that they are allowing Jesus to be Lord of their lives. What does our relationship with Jesus have to be if he truly is Lord of our lives? What does it mean to let Jesus be in charge?**

2. KING CATCHES ALL

Before the session, select certain cards from the deck. With a sharp permanent marker, write a Scripture reference on back of each card you selected: Psalm 1:6; Psalm 4:8; Psalm 9:9, 10; Psalm 23:1; Psalm 135:5, 6; Psalm 146:10; Proverbs 19:21; Isaiah 6:1-3; Isaiah 45:22-24; Acts 17:24. Place these cards back in the deck.

MATERIALS
a deck of playing cards, a Bible

DO: Students should sit in a circle on the floor or around a table. Shuffle the cards and deal them facedown to each student, so that all students have a stack of cards, facedown, in front of them. They may not look at the front of the cards. Choose one person to begin play. This person turns over the first card in his stack and lays it in the center. If it is a king, he keeps the card, and if it has a Scripture on back, he (because he's the king), gets to choose another student to look up the Scripture and read it. If his card is not a king, the person to his left turns over her top card and places it on top of the first card in the center. Play continues moving to the left with each person placing a card on the stack. If a king is played, the person playing the king takes all the cards in the stack, looks on the backs of the cards, and if there are any Scriptures written on them, chooses who will look up and read each Scripture. The cards taken by the king are added to the stack of the student who played the king. They are placed facedown under his original stack. Then play continues until someone is out of cards.

DISCUSS: After a Scripture has been read, ask: **What does that verse tell you about the Lord and his authority?** Say: **The word "Lord" can also mean "king." What kind of authority does a king have? What it is about our Lord that is kingly? What does it mean for Jesus to be the King of your life?**

3. ME, SIR?

DO: Choose one student to be the king. The others form a line and number off, one, two, three, and so on. The king says, "I, the king, have lost my hat. Number 4 (or any number he chooses) knows where it's at." The student with the number he has called answers, "Who, sir, me, sir? No, not I, sir. Number 1, sir" (or any number he chooses). The student whose number was called immediately says, "Who, sir, me, sir? No, not I, sir. Number 3, sir" (or any number he chooses). Anyone who doesn't immediately say his line after his number is called must move to the end of the line. That makes the numbers change. The king begins again, "I, the king, have lost my hat . . ." and the

MATERIALS

game goes on. You can pause the game at any time and let student number 1 become the king. Everyone moves up a place, and the king takes the place at the end of the line.

DISCUSS: Ask: **What is the word of respect that we are using to address the king?** (The king is being called "sir.") Ask students to list other words used to address people who are in authority (your majesty, officer, your honor). Ask: **Why is it important to address or greet these people in this way? How should we address the Lord?** Choose some students to read aloud Matthew 6:9; Galatians 4:6; and Exodus 20:7. Ask: **What do these Scriptures tell us about talking to and about the Lord? What does it mean to allow Jesus to be the Lord of your life?**

DISCOVERERS' DEBRIEFING

If you have time to review, gather as a large group and discuss your young discoverers' findings. Ask the following questions:
- **What is the most interesting thing you discovered today?**
- **What did you learn today that you did not know before?**
- **What does "Lord" mean when it's written in all capital letters?**
- **What does it mean when only the L is capitalized?**
- **What is the relationship a person must have with God and Jesus in order to call them "Lord?"**
- **What does it mean to let Jesus be the Lord of your life?**

Review the Scripture for today.

Pray, thanking God that he is strong and wise and worthy to be our Lord and King. Ask him to help us learn more about what it means to let him be in charge.

Insignias

U.S. Army

General of the Army

General

Lieutenant General

Major General

Brigadier General

Colonel

Major

Captain

Lieutenant

First Sergeant

Corporal

Private

U.S. Navy

Fleet Admiral

Admiral

Vice-Admiral

Rear Admiral

Commodore

Captain

Commander

Lieutenant Commander

Lieutenant

Lieutenant Junior Grade

Ensign

The Fear of the Lord

Scripture

"Fear of the Lord gives life, security, and protection from harm." Proverbs 19:23, NLT

Goal

Learn that fear of the Lord means awe, respect, and fear.

INTRODUCTION

Before the session, make one copy per student of Beginnings sheet (page 20). Then make one copy of Titles (page 19). Cut apart the titles. Staple or tape each title onto a different piece of construction paper. Post the titles around the room. As students arrive, team them up into pairs. Give each pair a copy of the Beginnings page and a pencil. Together, the partners try to match the beginnings of the books to their titles.

DISCOVERY RALLY

Gather the students together in a large group.

WHAT'S THE GOOD WORD?

Choose a student to read the Scripture for the day.

THE CHALLENGE

Read the answers to the Titles and Beginnings activity. Say: **If someday your life story was written in a book, and if you wanted that book to show that you were wise, then I wonder what the beginning would be?** Ask a student to read Psalm 111:10. Ask another student to read Proverbs 9:10. Ask: **What is the beginning of a wise life?** Tell the students that in their Discovery Centers today they will discover what it means to fear the Lord.

PRAYER

DISCOVERY CENTERS

1. NATURAL DISASTERS

DO: Choose one student to be the Timer, and give him a stopwatch. Choose another student to be the Clue-giver. The Clue-giver draws a card. Tell the students that the words on the cards are natural disasters. When the Timer says, "Go," the Clue-giver begins giving one-word clues for the word on her card. The other students try to guess within two minutes what the wonder is. The Clue-giver can give as many clues as she wants, as long as the clues are only one word, like "wind. . .cloud. . .whirl. . .crash. . ." The student who guesses correctly gets to be the next Clue-giver. However, if no one guesses correctly, the Timer calls, "Time" when two minutes is up. Then the Clue-giver tells the word on her card and chooses another student to become the Clue-giver.

MATERIALS

a Bible, a stopwatch, a pencil, a piece of paper, index cards with one natural wonder written on each: tornado, hurricane, hail, blizzard, volcano, earthquake, flood, lightning, avalanche, sandstorm, quicksand

DISCUSS: Tell the students that most people fear natural disasters. Ask them why. Say: **Natural disasters are powerful. They are not completely predictable; in other words, people never know exactly what will happen when these disasters occur. We take warnings of these disasters seriously. Are any of these natural disasters more powerful than God? God is much more powerful. And he is not completely predictable.** Ask someone to read Exodus 3:1-6. Ask: **Why did Moses hide his face? Fearing God can mean being truly afraid of God. But all through the Bible, God tells us that he loves and cares for us.** Ask someone to read Genesis 15:1. Say: **For those of us who love God, fearing God doesn't mean being terrified of him. But it does means taking God seriously.**

2. LIGHTNING ART

DO: Give each student a piece of black paper and a straw. Let students pour a nickel-sized spot of yellow paint onto the center of their paper. Then ask them to gently blow through their straws onto the paint, causing it to zigzag out from the center in lines that look like lightning.

MATERIALS
black construction paper, drinking straws, yellow washable liquid paint, a Bible

DISCUSS: While the students work, ask them to describe how they feel when they see lightning. Say: **Lightning is beautiful and exciting. It's electricity, and we depend on electricity for many of the things we do.** Ask: **Why is it good to have a healthy fear of lightning and electricity?** Read Luke 8:22-25. Ask: **What did the disciples feel after Jesus stilled the storm? Why did they feel that way? Fear of the Lord includes the feeling of awe and amazement at who he is and what he does. It means respecting him and taking him seriously.**

3. THE KEY WORD

DO: Give each student a pencil and a copy of the Key Word page. Tell them that they are to think of things that

MATERIALS
one copy for each student of The Key Word (page 21), pencils, a timer or stopwatch

God is Lord over. You will give them three minutes to write down as many things as they can think of. (This includes anything.) But these things must start with L, O, R, or D. Words starting with L should be written in a column under the L on the page. O words go under the O, and so on. Tell the students when to start. After five minutes, call time. Then ask one student to read all the L words she thought of. Everyone who wrote down this word must raise their hands and cross out that word on their list. The one reading the word also crosses it out, unless no one else thought of that word. Continue around the circle, with each person reading the L words from their list that are not crossed out. Then choose another person to read words from the O column. Continue in this way until all words have been read. The person with the most words that are not crossed out wins.

DISCUSS: Ask someone to read aloud the Scripture at the bottom of the page. Ask: **What does "the fear of the Lord" mean here? It means respecting God and taking him seriously. Why would that be the key to salvation? Why would that be the key to wisdom and knowledge? Why is the Lord worthy of our respect? How can we show respect for the Lord?**

DISCOVERERS' DEBRIEFING

If you have time to review, gather as a large group and discuss your young discoverers' findings. Ask the following questions:
- **What is the most interesting thing you discovered today?**
- **What did you learn today that you did not know before?**
- **What is the key to wisdom and knowledge?**
- **What is the fear of the Lord?**
- **How can we show that we respect the Lord and take him seriously?**

Review the Scripture for today.

Pray, praising God for his great power and wisdom. Thank him for being a good, caring God. Ask him to help you always to remember how awesome he is, and always to take him seriously.

Titles

1

LITTLE HOUSE ON THE PRAIRIE

by Laura Ingalls Wilder

2

WHERE THE WILD THINGS ARE

by Maurice Sendak

3

MAKE WAY FOR DUCKLINGS

by Robert McCloskey

4

MADELINE

by Ludwig Bemelmans

5

THE BEST CHRISTMAS PAGEANT EVER

by Barbara Robinson

6

HENRY AND RIBSY

by Beverly Cleary

7

ENCYCLOPEDIA BROWN BOY DETECTIVE

by Donald J. Sobel

8

THE WONDERFUL WIZARD OF OZ

by L. Frank Baum

9

THE LION, THE WITCH,
AND THE WARDROBE

by C.S. Lewis

10

THE BIBLE

Beginnings

Each of the sayings below is the beginning of a book. Find the book that you think the beginning came from, and write the number of the book in the blank.

_____ "One warm Saturday morning in August, Henry Huggins and his mother and father were eating breakfast in their square white house on Klickitat Street."

_____ "The Herdmans were absolutely the worst kids in the history of the world."

_____ "In the beginning God created the heavens and the earth."

_____ "A long time ago, when all grandfathers and grandmothers of today were little boys and little girls or very small babies, or perhaps not even born, Pa and Ma and Mary and Laura and Baby Carrie left their little house in the Big Woods of Wisconsin."

_____ "Mr. and Mrs. Brown had one child. They called him Leroy, and so did his teachers."

_____ "Dorothy lived in the midst of the great Kansas prairies, with Uncle Henry, who was a farmer, and Aunt Em, who was the farmer's wife.

_____ "The night Max wore his wolf suit and made mischief of one kind and another his mother called him "WILD THING!" and . . . he was sent to bed without eating anything."

_____ "In an old house in Paris that was covered with vines lived twelve little girls in two straight lines."

_____ "Once there were four children whose names were Peter, Susan, Edmund and Lucy."

_____ "Mr. and Mrs. Mallard were looking for a place to live. But every time Mr. Mallard saw what looked like a nice place, Mrs. Mallard said it was no good."

The Key Word

L	O	R	D

"The fear of the Lord is the key to the treasures of
salvation, wisdom and knowledge" (Isaiah 33:6, NLT).

Lord Over Leaders

Scripture
"For the Lord is king! He rules all the nations."
Psalm 22:28, NLT

Goal
Learn that God rules as Lord over leaders and nations.

INTRODUCTION

Copy one page per student of Famous Bible Leaders (page 27). As students arrive, give a pencil and a Bible Leaders page to each one. Encourage them to solve the puzzles to find out who the famous leaders are.

DISCOVERY RALLY

Gather the students together in a large group.

WHAT'S THE GOOD WORD?
Choose a student to read the Scripture for the day.

THE CHALLENGE

Ask students to name some of the leaders they discovered in the introductory activity. Tell them that the most famous Bible leader of all wasn't even on the page. Ask them to guess who it is. It's Jesus. Ask: **Was Jesus a leader only in Bible times?** Say: **Jesus continues to lead us today. He is Lord.** Review by asking what "Lord" means. Then tell students that in their Discovery Centers today they will find out more about this King who rules all other kings.

PRAYER

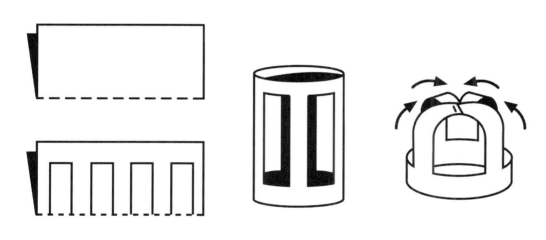

DISCOVERY CENTERS

1. CROWNS AND DIADEMS

DO: Give each student a strip of interfacing. Students should fold their interfacing in half lengthwise and cut as shown in the diagram. After opening the interfacing again, students write across the bottom border, "God, the blessed and only Ruler, the King of kings and Lord of lords" (1 Timothy 6:15). Then they staple the short ends of the interfacing together to make a cylinder. Working on the top of the cylinder, bring the four sides together at the top, placing one on top of the other as shown. Then staple

MATERIALS
a Bible, one 9" x 22" strip of stiff fabric backing or interfacing for each student, scissors, markers, stapler and staples, flat adhesive-backed costume jewels from a craft store (optional)

these together. This makes the crown. Let students decorate their crowns with drawn designs or adhesive-backed "jewels."

DISCUSS: As students work, tell them that the word "crown" and the word "diadem" are both used to describe the head covering worn by someone in authority. A turban was the first kind of diadem talked about in the Bible. Ask students to describe a turban. Say: **Turbans were worn by priests in bible times. The Hebrew word that describes the crown that Esther wore really means "turban." Diadems and crowns are symbols of authority and power.** Ask: **Who is the most powerful ruler? Who has all authority?** Then ask someone to read Matthew 27:27-29, 35-37. Ask: **What kind of crown did the soldiers give Jesus? Why? If they had known who Jesus really was, what kind of crown would they have given him?** Ask students to read the verse across the border of their crowns. Ask: **What does "King of kings and Lord of lords" mean?" It means that God is greater than all kings and lords here on earth. He has more power and greater authority. Kings and queens, lords and rulers, presidents and prime ministers should bow before God.**

2. WORLD LEADERS

Before the session, tape or tack the butcher paper to a wall, one section above the other to make a large square. In pencil, draw a general outline of a world map on this square. From the magazines or newspapers tear out any pages that would not be appropriate for your students to see.

MATERIALS
a Bible, news magazines and newspapers that show pictures of national and international leaders, scissors, butcher paper cut into three six-foot lengths, tape, crayons

DO: Your first group should trace over the map outline and color in the continents and ocean. Choose someone in group #1 to write at the top of the map, "O Lord, you rule over all the kingdoms of the nations (2 Chronicles 20:6)." If this first group has time, they can then follow the directions for your second and third groups. These groups cut out headlines and pictures about events and leaders in our nation and other nations. Then they tape these headlines and pictures onto the areas of the world map where they happened. Choose someone in group #2 to write at the bottom of the map, "The Lord upsets the plans of the nations (Psalm 33:10)." Choose someone in group #3 to write on an ocean space, "The Most High rules over the kingdoms of the world and gives them to anyone he chooses (Daniel 4:25)."

DISCUSS: As the students work, challenge them to think about who is in charge in each of the situations described by their headlines and pictures. Ask: **Is there any situation here which is out of God's control?** Read John 19:5-11. Ask: **Who gave Pilate his power? Who has authority over the whole earth? What does it mean for the Lord to have authority over the whole earth?**

3. PRAYER STARTER

MATERIALS
one 9" x 9" square of paper for each student, pens or markers, a Bible

DO: Give each student a square of paper and a pen or marker. Direct them to fold one corner of the square to the other corner and crease the fold. Open the square. Then fold the other two corners together and crease. Open the square again. There will be an X marked on the square from the creases. Students should now fold each corner to the center of the X and leave these folds in place as shown. Turn this new square over and fold each corner to the center again. Turn this square over. Place left pointer finger and thumb into two adjacent flaps. Place the right pointer finger and thumb into the other two flaps. Bring all four flaps together into a point as shown. Now ask the students to name people who are in positions of authority. These can be from family, school, organizations, local, national and international authorities. Each student chooses eight people in authority and writes those eight names or positions on the eight inside flaps of the prayer starter. Call out a number from 1 to 10. The students open and close the prayer starter that many times and then pray for one of the four names or positions that is revealed inside.

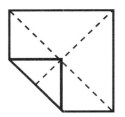
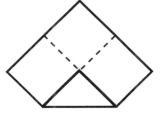

DISCUSS: Ask someone to read Psalm 75:7. Point out that putting people in positions of authority is something God can do because he is Lord, the ruler, the greatest authority. Ask someone to read 2 Chronicles 36:22, 23. Ask how God showed his authority in King Cyrus. Ask someone to read Daniel 2:20, 21. Ask: **Who sets up kings and removes kings? Does this mean only kings, or does it mean other rulers and leaders as well?** Now ask someone to read 1 Timothy 2:1, 2. Ask: **What is our responsibility to those in authority over us? Why should we pray for our leaders?**

DISCOVERERS' DEBRIEFING

If you have time to review, gather as a large group and discuss your young discoverers' findings. Ask the following questions:

• **What is the most interesting thing you discovered today?**
• **What did you learn today that you did not know before?**
• **What is God's position in relation to kings and other leaders?**
• **What is God's position in relation to the nations of the world?**
• **What is our responsibility toward those in authority over us?**

Review the Scripture for today.

Pray, thanking God for being the King over all kings and the Lord over all lords. Pray for your nation and the leaders of your nation.

Famous Bible Leaders

1. Cross out the letters below that spell LEADER and you will find the name of one of the most famous leaders in the Bible. Write his name in the blanks.

L E M A O D S E E R S

☐☐☐☐☐

2. Cross out the letters that spell KING and you will find the name of one of the most famous kings in the Bible. Write his name in the blanks.

K D I A N V I G D

☐☐☐☐☐

3. Cross out the letters that spell QUEEN and you will find the name of one of the most famous queens in the Bible. Write her name in the blanks.

Q E U S E E T N H E R

☐☐☐☐☐☐

4. Cross out the letters that spell RULER and you will find the name of one of the smartest kings in the world. Write his name in the blanks.

S R O U L L O E M R O N

☐☐☐☐☐☐☐

5. Cross out the letters that spell POWER and you will find the name of a woman who led God's people. Write her name in the blanks.

P D O E B W O R E A H R

☐☐☐☐☐☐☐

Jesus Is Lord

Scripture

"Now he sits on the throne of highest honor in heaven, at God's right hand. . . . God has made this Jesus whom you crucified to be both Lord and Messiah!" Acts 2:33, 36, NLT

Goal

Learn that God gave Jesus the authority of Lordship.

INTRODUCTION

As students arrive, divide them into pairs. Give each pair a pencil and a copy of Measure Up! (page 34). Have available a carpenter's plumb line and level, a measuring tape, a yardstick, and a ruler. (You may need more than one of each if you have a large class.) Ask the students to find the answers to the measuring challenges on the Measure Up! page.

DISCOVERY RALLY

Gather the students together in a large group.

WHAT'S THE GOOD WORD?

Choose a student to read the Scripture for the day.

THE CHALLENGE

Hold up the plumb line. Tell the students that plumb lines have been used since Old Testament times, long before Jesus was born. Say: **A plumb is an easy tool to make. It's simply a string or cord with a weight at the bottom of it. In ancient times, when people were building a wall, they would dangle a plumb line in the air beside the wall to make sure they were building it straight. Builders today still use plumb lines to make sure that what they build is straight. What would happen if walls were not built straight? Have you heard of the Tower of Pisa? Why is it famous? It leans about 17 feet out of line, and it leans about 1/4" more each year! What will happen to it if it keeps leaning?**

Now ask: **If I said that Jesus is like our plumb line, what do you think that would mean?** After some discussion, say: **Jesus is the standard by which we measure everything else in life. We can say that if it's something Jesus would do, we can do it. If it's something Jesus would not do, then we can't do it. It won't bring us peace and joy.** Then tell the students that in their Discovery Centers today they will find out why it's so important that Jesus is Lord.

PRAYER

DISCOVERY CENTERS

1. STICKY NOTE TIME LINE

DO: Place the butcher paper horizontally on a wall or floor. Choose a student to draw a horizontal line with a

> **MATERIALS**
> a four-foot length of butcher paper, non-permanent markers, Bibles, large 2 7/8" x 2 7/8" sticky postable notes, pens or pencils

marker across the center of the paper from left to right. Choose another student to draw a cross on this line in the very center. Now assign different Scriptures for the students to look up from these categories:

1. Use at least one of these: Genesis 2:7; Exodus 33:18, 19; Judges 2:16; 1 Samuel 2:1; Ezra 3:11; Psalm 8:1; Proverbs 1:7; Daniel 2:47.
2. Use at least one of these: Matthew 8:25; Matthew 14:28; Matthew 20:33; Mark 11:9
3. Use all of these: John 6:15; Luke 18:33, 34; Acts 1:6.
4. Use at least one of these: Hebrews 1:3; Romans 10:9; 2 Corinthians 4:5.

Choose students with verses in category #1 to read aloud their assigned verses. As each student reads a verse, ask which person or event is related to that verse. (For example, for Genesis 2 the person would be Adam or the event Creation.) On a sticky note, the student writes the name of that person or event. Your group can help the student decide where to place that event on the time line. If it's before Jesus' death, it will go before the cross. Ask the group: **Who is being referred to as "Lord" in this Scripture: God or Jesus?**

Now ask for readings from category #2. Those sticky notes should be placed on the time line. Question the students as suggested above.

Ask for readings from category #3. Those sticky notes should be placed on the time line. Question students as suggested above. But this time, ask: **Did the people really understand the kind of Lord that Jesus was? What kind of Lord did they think he would be?** (They thought he would be an earthly king.)

Ask for readings from category #4. Those sticky notes should be placed on the time line. Question students as before. Then ask: **Is there anything different about what Paul means when he says, "Jesus is Lord"?** (Paul means that Jesus is Ruler of heaven and earth just as God the Father is.)

DISCUSS: Try to help the students understand that, of course, no one in Old Testament times knew of Jesus as Lord, because he hadn't come yet. And when Jesus came, no one really thought of Jesus as being Lord over all until Jesus went back to heaven. Point out that when people realized that God had really put Jesus in charge, it was as if a light turned on in their minds. They could say, "Now I get it!" And it was one of the most exciting things for the first Christians to realize: Jesus is Lord!

2. THE SIGN

MATERIALS

copies of the Semaphore page (page 35), two 8 1/2" x 8 1/2" squares of white paper and one of black paper for each student, scissors, glue

DO: Give each student a Semaphore page, two squares of white paper, and one square of black paper. Ask them to fold one corner of the black paper to its opposite corner to make a triangle. Then they should cut along the fold line. Now they glue one black triangle onto one white square, matching corners and sides. They do the same on the other white square. Ask them to see if they can make the semaphore signs that spell JESUS. Practice it together. Try LORD.

DISCUSS: After you've practiced Semaphore signals, ask students to name some other ways to communicate that Jesus is Lord. Then hold up your pointer finger, middle finger and ring finger together. Tell students that this means "Jesus is Lord." Say: **Knowing that Jesus is Lord is one of the most important things we'll ever know. Telling others that Jesus is Lord is one of the most important things we'll ever communicate. Why? What does it mean for Jesus to be Lord?** (He's in charge, so you don't have to worry. He directs. He is your standard. His words and teachings guide your life. You do things his way. He's the most important thing in your life.)

3. DOOR KNOB HANGERS

MATERIALS

a Bible, a variety of colors of felt cut into 4" x 8" rectangles, pencils, small bathroom-sized paper cups, scissors, fabric markers or fabric paints, glue, sparkly or glittery rickrack

DO: Give each student a felt rectangle, pencil, and paper cup. Ask the students to turn the paper cup upside down in the center of the top half of the rectangle and trace around it with a pencil. Then cut the circle out. To start the cut-out, fold the rectangle in half lengthwise and make a cut through both layers of felt within the traced circle area. The resulting hole

will slip over a doorknob. In the bottom portion of the felt, ask the children to write "JESUS IS LORD" with markers or paint. Students can further decorate the door hanger with more paint or with rickrack glued onto the felt.

DISCUSS: Remind the students that God had been called Lord from the very beginning of time. Ask: **What do you think it meant to people in Jesus' time when they heard people call Jesus "Lord"?** Ask someone to read Colossians 1:15-19. Ask: **What does it mean for Jesus to be your Lord?** (He's in charge, so you don't have to worry. He directs. He is your standard. His words and teachings guide your life. You do things his way. He's the most important thing in your life.) Tell the students that a pro football player once said it this way: "When I go to bed at night, I don't lie awake worrying about problems, because there's somebody working on it while I'm asleep!" Encourage the students to put these door hangers on the doorknobs of their bedrooms to remind them of the one who can guide and guard their lives, even while they sleep.

DISCOVERERS' DEBRIEFING

If you have time to review, gather as a large group and discuss your young discoverers' findings. Ask the following questions:

- **What is the most interesting thing you discovered today?**
- **What did you learn today that you did not know before?**
- **What does it mean to say that Jesus is like our plumb line?**
- **Before Jesus came, who did people call "Lord"?**
- **What kind of king did people think Jesus was going to be?**

- **What very important truth did people realize about Jesus after he went back to heaven?**
- **What does it mean in your life today to call Jesus "Lord"?**

Review the Scripture for today.

Pray, thanking God for his plan to make Jesus Lord of all. Ask God to help us understand more of what it means to let Jesus be in charge of our lives.

Measure Up!

With a partner, see what you can discover by measuring. Do the following experiments in any order you wish.

- Use a plumb line. If you don't know what it is, ask a classmate or teacher. When you've discovered how to use it, test door frames, window frames, desk and table legs, and even the corners of your room. Are they straight?

- Use a level. You can find out what a level is and how to use one by asking a classmate or teacher. Then use it to test surfaces in your classroom: tables, window sills, desks, chalk boards. Are they level?

- Use a yardstick or measuring tape. Hold your arms straight out sideways. Ask your partner to measure your arm span. Now measure your partner's arm span. Then measure each other's height.
  Partner #1 arm span: _____ Height _____
  Partner #2 arm span: _____ Height _____
  What did you discover?

- Use a ruler to measure the length of your feet. Now measure the length of the inside of your arm from the bend of your elbow to your wrist.
  Partner #1 foot length: _____ Inner arm length: _____
  Partner #2 foot length: _____ Inner arm length: _____
  What did you discover?

- Use a ruler to measure the length of your hand from wrist to tip of middle finger. Now measure the length of your face from chin to hairline above the forehead.
  Partner #1 hand length: _____ Face length: _____
  Partner #2 hand length: _____ Face length: _____
  What did you discover?

Semaphores

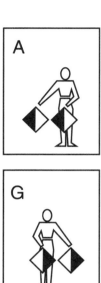 A

B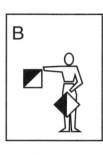

C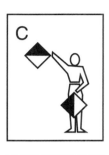

D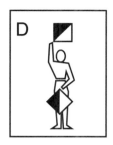

E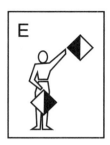

F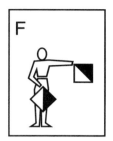

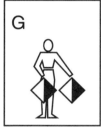 G

 H

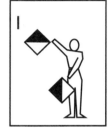 I

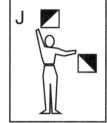 J

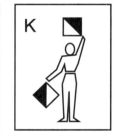 K

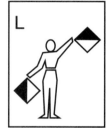 L

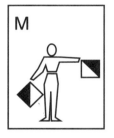 M

 N

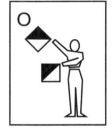 O

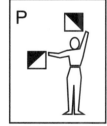 P

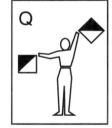 Q

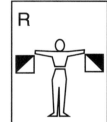 R

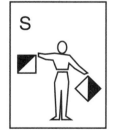 S

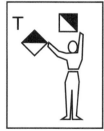 T

 U

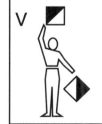 V

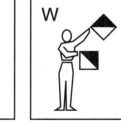 W

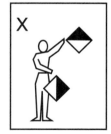 X

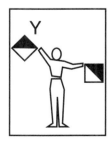 Y

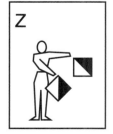 Z

Authority Over Sin

Scripture

"I will prove that I, the Son of Man, have the authority on earth to forgive sins." Mark 2:10, NLT

Goal

Learn that Jesus' Lordship includes the authority to forgive sins.

INTRODUCTION

Before the session, gather products, containers, or ads that contain the symbols for the "Good Housekeeping Seal of Approval," the "Parent's Choice" approval, the "FDA Inspected" approval, and any other approval symbol you find. You may include some well-known product logos as well. Set these out for the students to look at as they arrive. Ask them to name some of the types of products that bear the symbols or logos they see. Ask students to imagine that they are in a position to give their approval to products. Their seal would be called "The (student's name) Seal of Approval."

Give students markers, crayons, and paper, and ask them to design their own seal of approval.

DISCOVERY RALLY

Gather the students together in a large group.

WHAT'S THE GOOD WORD?

Choose a student to read the Scripture for the day.

THE CHALLENGE

Let the students show the seals they have designed. Show any seals of approval you brought. Ask: **What does a seal of approval mean? It means that the product passes the standards for good quality that are set by the group who gives the seal. Every time we see that seal, we know we can trust that the product is good. If the seal says it's good, it's good. The group that gives the seal has an authority, an understanding or knowledge, that people trust.**

Tell the students that God has a seal of approval that he wants to place in our lives: Jesus. When we ask Jesus to be our Lord and Savior, God makes us pure and gives us his approval. Tell the students that in their Discovery Centers today, they will find out more about the authority of Jesus' Lordship to forgive our sins.

PRAYER

DISCOVERY CENTERS

1. AT JESUS' FEET

DO: Mark an X on the floor with masking tape, and set the step stool about a foot away from the X. Give each student a piece of paper. Students take turns standing on the step stool and trying to drop the paper so that it lands exactly on the X. (A teacher should stand close by in case there's a need to steady the student.) After each student has had a turn, let students punch two

MATERIALS

a Bible, masking tape, a hole puncher, two 5' lengths of string and a piece of paper for each student, and one step stool, short ladder, or sturdy chair holes in their papers, one at each end of the paper. Then they tie a string in each hole. Now they may take turns lowering the paper onto the X from the step stool. After they've all had a turn, ask someone to read Mark 2:1-12.

DISCUSS: Ask: **Was it easier for the paper to land on the X with or without the strings? Why?** Say: **In the reading, the four friends lowered the sick man right in front of Jesus. How do you think they knew where to dig the hole in the roof and where to let their friend down? What did Jesus say? How did Jesus prove to the people that he had the authority to forgive sins? Why did Jesus have the authority to forgive sins? Who has the authority to forgive sins today? Forgiving sins is part of the authority that Jesus has because he is Lord.**

2. CRUMPLED PAPER

DO: Before the session, place a fresh sheet of paper inside the empty trash can. To begin the session, hold up another piece of paper, and ask the students to look at it and describe it. It is smooth and flat. Say: **Let's imagine that this is a person's life. Is anyone perfect, never sinning?** Crumple one corner of the paper. Say: **Let's imagine that this is what sin does to this person's life. It messes things up.** Ask the students to name some sins that students their age might do. Say: **But people don't sin just once in life. We sin again and again.** Crumple the paper more and more as you continue to talk. **Even when we try to do right, we sometimes make wrong choices. In fact, it may seem as if our whole lives are messed up with sin.** Crumple the whole sheet of paper into a ball. **Lots of people try to straighten out their own lives.** Ask a student to smooth out the paper again and give it back to you. Show it to everyone. **Does it look the way it did when we began? No. It's wrinkled. People can't ever make up for their own sins. Some people get so discouraged, they say, "There's no hope. My life is trashed. It's garbage. I've thrown away my life."** Throw the ball of paper into the trash can. **But if we ask Jesus to be our Lord**—reach into the trash can and pull out a fresh sheet of paper—**then he forgives our sins and makes our lives spotless, fresh, and clean.**

Now give each student a piece of paper and set the remaining stack of paper beside the trash can. Ask the students to crumple their papers. As they do, ask them to retell the object lesson you just told. Now, one at a time, each student tosses the paper into the trash can, and picks up a fresh piece. On this fresh piece, they write the Scripture for the day, Mark 2:10, quoted above.

DISCUSS: As the students write the verse, explain that Jesus has the authority to forgive sins, because he is Lord. He made us, and he can remake us.

3. A CLEAN HEART

DO: Give each student a yellow crayon and a piece of paper. Ask them to draw a large heart shape that covers most of the paper. Then ask them to write the first part of Psalm 51:10 inside the heart: "Create in me a clean heart, O God." Then give each student a piece of red cellophane or report cover. Ask students to use the black marker to draw a large heart on this red sheet. Ask the students to lay the red sheet over the paper. The yellow heart is no longer visible. Ask someone to read Acts 13:38.

DISCUSS: Ask if anyone knows what a "pardon" is. To pardon someone is to set that person free from the punishment for his crimes. The person who is pardoned is completely free. He is no longer considered a criminal. The pardon erases his conviction. But the pardon has to be given by someone in authority like a governor or king or president. President George Washington pardoned a group of farmers who had been convicted of not paying taxes on their crops. President Andrew Johnson pardoned most of the Southerners for fighting against the Northern States in the Civil War. But one of the most famous pardons is told about in the Bible. Ask someone to read Matthew 27:15-26. Remind students that a person who pardons another person cannot really make them sinless before God. Only Jesus has the authority of Lordship. Only he has the power to erase our sins.

Discoverers' Debriefing
Discoverers' Debriefing

DISCOVERERS' DEBRIEFING

If you have time to review, gather as a large group and discuss your young discoverers' findings. Ask the following questions:

- **What is the most interesting thing you discovered today?**
- **What did you learn today that you did not know before?**
- **How did Jesus prove that he had the authority to forgive sins?**
- **Why can't people straighten out their own lives and get rid of sin?**
- **What is a pardon? Who gives it? Who pardons us of sin?**
- **Why does Jesus have the authority to forgive sins?**

Review the Scripture for today.

Pray, thanking God for making Jesus our Lord and giving him the authority to forgive our sins.

The Way and the Truth

Scripture

*"Jesus told him, 'I am the way and the truth . . .
No one can come to the Father except through me.'"
John 14:6, NIV*

Goal

*Learn that Jesus' Lordship includes being the only way to God
the Father. Learn that Jesus' Lordship includes being not a truth,
but the Truth.*

INTRODUCTION

As students arrive, give each one a pencil and a copy of the Backwards page
(page 46). Ask them to write the words on the page backwards to find out
what they spell.

DISCOVERY RALLY

Gather the students together in a large group.

WHAT'S THE GOOD WORD?

Choose a student to read the Scripture for the day.

THE CHALLENGE

Ask for volunteers to tell some of the words that they discovered that spelled something backward as well as forward. Ask if any of them has a name that spells something when read backward. Then on a chalkboard, dry erase board, or poster board, write "LIVE." Ask what it spells backward. Say: **This word has a very important truth in it: Life lived backward (or the wrong way) is evil. Life lived the right way is full of joy and peace, even in times of trouble.**

Then tell the students that in their Discovery Centers today they will find out more about Jesus as Lord. He is the Way and the Truth.

PRAYER

DISCOVERY CENTERS

1. BLIND ON THE PATHWAY

DO: You may do this activity indoors or outdoors. Divide the group into pairs. One student in each pair wears a blindfold. The other student is the guide. Have the students take a walk. The guide tells the blindfolded student when to walk straight ahead, turn left, turn right, slow down and so on. The guide's job is to get his partner through the walk without bumping into anything. Then the students switch roles, and they take a walk again.

MATERIALS
a blindfold for half of the students

DISCUSS: When the students have completed their walks, tell them this story: There was once man who was exploring Africa. He had an African guide who was leading him through a jungle where there were no trails. They had walked for a long time, and the explorer began to worry about getting lost. "Is this the way?" asked the explorer. The guide said, "There is no way. I am the way." Ask the students what the guide meant. There was no path, so the explorer had to trust the guide. The guide was the only way through the jungle. Ask if they experienced something like that when they walked blindfolded. Say: When you were blindfolded, the way was not a path, it was a person. So what do you think Jesus meant when he said, "I am the way"? Jesus' Lordship includes being the Way to a right relationship with God.

2. OWNER'S MANUAL

DO: Ask the students to look over the manuals and tell you what they think these manuals are for. Ask: **Why does an appliance, computer, or car come with instructions? What happens if people ignore the instructions? The manual tells you the way that the maker of the product made it to work best. In many cases, if something breaks, the maker won't replace it if you've used it in the wrong way.**

> **MATERIALS**
> owner's operating manuals for appliances, computer, car, etc., one or more Bibles that have "Holy Bible" embossed on the front, paper, crayons

Now give each student a piece of paper and crayon. Ask them to write across the bottom of the paper, "Owner's Manual for Me." Then pass the Bible(s) around. Ask each student to place the paper over the embossed title and rub over it with a crayon. "Holy Bible" will appear on the paper.

DISCUSS: Ask: **How is the Bible like an owner's operating manual?** Say: **God made us, and he knows how life works best for us. God's way is the Way. It's the way to think, the way to act, the way to feel, the way to live. E. Stanley Jones, a missionary to India once said, "There are just two things in life—the Way or not-the-way"** (*The Unshakable Kingdom and the Unchanging Person*, Abingdon Press, 1972). **If sin were the way to a great life, then we should sin in all we do. We'd have happy, peaceful lives, right?**

Wrong. That's not the way life works. Sin leads to trouble. Jesus is Lord, so he is the Way, and the Bible is the operating manual for our lives.

3. TRUTH IN THE WORLD

DO: Give each students a handful of toothpicks. Tell them you will give them codes that people use every day, and they are to show that code using their toothpicks. Practice by giving the code 2 + 2. They should place two toothpicks on the table in front of them, leave a blank space, and place two more toothpicks. This represents the code. Give the code 3 x 3 (if some need help, clarify that this means 3 toothpicks three times.) Continue to call out simple addition and multiplication codes, being careful to encourage and help those who may need explanation. This will depend on the age and abilities of your group.

After the students have practiced several math codes, give each student a paper plate and some play dough. Ask them to flatten the dough onto the plate to make a tablet. On the dough tablet, they should use a toothpick to write, "Jesus, the Truth." Then they should lay two toothpicks on top of the left side of the dough and two toothpicks on the right side of the dough. They gently press these four toothpicks into the dough to become part of the design.

DISCUSS: Lay out two toothpicks plus two more toothpicks. Say: **What if I said, "2 + 2 = 3"? Would that be true? How do you know? Does 2 + 2 ever equal 3? Why? We call these truths "facts." Once you know that 2 + 2 = 4 is true, then you depend on it. How do we depend on math truths? Buying, selling, telling time, measuring. But what if we couldn't agree on what 2 + 2 really is? What if some people said, "2 + 2 = 4 may be a truth for you, but 2 + 2 = 5 is the truth for me"? Could we buy and sell, tell time, measure things? Why not? Two plus two is not one of many truths about 2 + 2, it's the truth about 2 + 2. In life, some people say there are many truths, and Jesus is one of them. What do you think Jesus meant when he said that he is the Truth? Jesus is the Truth for all people and all time.** Ask someone to read Colossians 1:15, 16. Say: **All true facts in the**

world depend on Jesus, because he created them. So if we want to know truth, we look at what Jesus said and how he lived. We can depend on 2 + 2 and build math on it. We can depend on Jesus and build our lives on him. He is Lord.

DISCOVERERS' DEBRIEFING

If you have time to review, gather as a large group and discuss your young discoverers' findings. Ask the following questions:

- **What is the most interesting thing you discovered today?**
- **What did you learn today that you did not know before?**
- **What did Jesus mean when he said, "I am the Way"?**
- **What is our owner's operating manual? Why?**
- **What did Jesus mean when he said, "I am the Truth"?**
- **What does "live" spell backwards? What message does that give us?**

Review the Scripture for today.

Pray, thanking God for showing us the Way in Jesus and the Truth in Jesus. Thank him for being our Lord.

The Backwards Page

Write these words backward to find what they spell.

lap	doom	net
star	reed	not
mug	trap	spot
slap	rat	tap
stab	won	tab
stop	pin	nap

The next words are a bit different. They are called palindromes. That means they spell the same thing backward and forward.

Bob	Nan	sis	eye
Ada	Eve	Hannah	noon
Otto	did	bib	radar

Here's a palindrome sentence. Read it backward.

Madam, I'm Adam.

The famous emperor Napoleon was thrown out of his country and forced to live in a place named Elba. This palindrome is supposed to be something that he said:

Able was I ere I saw Elba.

The Life

Scripture

"Jesus told him, 'I am the way and the truth and the life. No one comes to the Father except through me." John 14:6, NIV

Goal

Learn that Jesus' Lordship includes the authority to give us eternal life.

INTRODUCTION

Have several shades of green paper available, as well as scissors and tape. As the students arrive, show them how to make an origami tree, and ask them to make their own. Fold a sheet of green paper in half. Cut along the fold. Then tape the short end of one piece to the short end of the other, making a long strip. Roll this strip of paper up loosely and tape this tube in place. Then cut a long fringe all around the top of the tube through all layers. From the bottom of the tube, push the inside layers part of the way out of the tube. Bend the fringes outward to make the tree. Challenge the students to make a forest together.

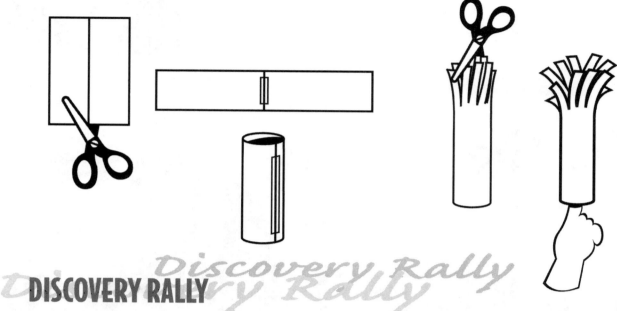

DISCOVERY RALLY

Gather the students together in a large group.

WHAT'S THE GOOD WORD?

Choose a student to read the Scripture for the day.

THE CHALLENGE

Ask the students to name some things that are not alive. Ask them to name some things that are alive. Ask: **How do you know something is alive?** (Things that are alive move, grow, and make other things like themselves—or reproduce). Say: **The time that something is alive is called its "life span." Which plants live longest?** (Scientists say that the bristlecone pine trees in the western United States live longest. There is a bristlecone pine still living that is believed to be 4,600 years old. That means it was more than 2,000 years old when Jesus was born!) **Which animal lives longest?** (Scientists say that giant tortoises can probably live as long as 200 years.) **Does anyone know the name of the person who lived the longest?** (Genesis 5:27 says that Methuselah lived 969 years. In recent history, the longest anyone has lived is about 120 years.) **But we can have eternal life. How long is eternity?**

Tell the students that in their Discovery Centers today they will find out more about Jesus as Lord. Jesus has the authority to give us eternal life.

PRAYER

DISCOVERY CENTERS

1. OUTLINES OF LIFE

MATERIALS
large pieces of manila paper, crayons
or markers, a Bible

DO: Give each student a piece of paper. Ask students to write "Life" in letters about 2" tall in the center of the paper. Then with one color of crayon or marker, they outline the word. With another color, they outline the first outline. They continue to outline each preceding outline with a different color until they've filled the page.

DISCUSS: As the students work, ask them to describe eternal life. Point out that eternal life is the length of life, and it's also the kind of life. If Jesus is our Savior, we are living part of our eternal life right now. Eternal life is life free from sin's power. It is life that is lived in a holy relationship: we as God's children, and God as our Father. It is life lived with help from God who cares for us and guides us. Ask someone to read John 10:10. Ask: **What do you think Jesus meant? What did he mean when he said, "I am the Life"?** (Jesus is the Lord, so he has the authority to give us eternal life.)

2. GROWING GREENERY

MATERIALS
one carrot with leaves for each student,
disposable paper or plastic bowls, knife (to
be used with close supervision), cutting
board, water, a Bible

DO: Give each student a bowl and a carrot. Ask them to name the parts of the carrot plant. Supervising closely, let each student cut off about 1/2" of the carrot top. Then they cut off the green leaves. (You should do the cutting if you feel that your students are not mature enough to do it safely.) Students should place the carrot tops in their bowls and add enough water to cover the carrot top halfway. Tell students to take these home and place them near a sunny window, but not in direct sunlight. They should make sure there's always enough water in the bowl. The carrot top should sprout in about a week.

DISCUSS: As students work, point out that it may look like they are destroying the carrot. But new green leaves will sprout again. Ask someone to read John 11:25. Ask: **What do you think Jesus meant?** Ask someone to read John 6:40. Ask your students what it means to them. Then say: **The carrot's leaves were cut off. But they will sprout and grow again. Our lives are a bit like the carrot top. Even if our bodies die, we have been given eternal life, so we'll be raised by Jesus to live forever with him, experiencing the wonders and greatness of heaven. Because Jesus is Lord, he has the authority to give us eternal life.**

3. WINDOW CROSS

DO: Spread old newspaper over the work surface. Give each student a piece of black construction paper. Ask them to draw a large cross on the paper and cut it out. Then they fold the cross in half lengthwise and use the hole punch and scissors to cut small shapes through both layers of the cross as shown. Set these aside. Give each student a large piece of white tissue paper to lay on the newspaper work surface. Let students mist the tissue paper with water from the spray bottle. (They should just dampen the paper and not soak it.) Then let students drip different colors of food coloring onto the damp tissue paper. Lay the cross

> **MATERIALS**
> old newspaper, white tissue paper, spray bottle of water, food coloring, black construction paper, scissors, hole puncher, string. stapler and staples, a Bible

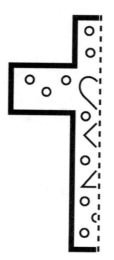

on top of the tissue paper and staple them together. Trim off the tissue paper that extends beyond the cross shape. Punch a hole in the top of the cross and tie a string through it for hanging.

DISCUSS: Ask: **Why would someone who is Lord of all allow himself to be killed on a cross like a lowly criminal?** Ask someone to read Romans 1:1-4. Ask: **When Jesus came back to life, what did that show about him?** (It showed he was truly the Son of God. He was the Lord.) Ask someone to read Ephesians 1:18-22. Ask: **What did God do after he raised Jesus from the dead? What authority does Jesus have now?** (Jesus is Lord. He has the authority to give us eternal life.) Ask someone to read Romans 10:9. Say: **God wants us to believe that he raised Jesus from the dead. But that's not all. What does God want us to confess or say?** (God wants us to confess that Jesus is Lord.)

DISCOVERERS' DEBRIEFING

If you have time to review, gather as a large group and discuss your young discoverers' findings. Ask the following questions:

- **What is the most interesting thing you discovered today?**
- **What did you learn today that you did not know before?**
- **What is eternal life?**
- **What did Jesus mean when he said, "I am the Life"?**
- **Why does Jesus have the authority to give us life?**
- **When Jesus came back to life, what did that show about him?**
- **God wants us to believe that he raised Jesus from the dead. What does God want us to confess (say) about Jesus?**

Review the Scripture for today.

Pray, thanking God for raising Jesus from the dead. Thank him for giving Jesus the authority to give us eternal life.

The Bread of Life

Scripture

"Jesus replied, 'I am the bread of life.'" John 6:35, NLT

Goal

*Learn that just as our bodies need nourishment,
so also our spirits need nourishment. Learn that Jesus'
Lordship includes the authority to nourish our spirits.*

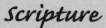

INTRODUCTION

Bring a variety of breads: whole wheat, rye, graham crackers, corn bread, oat bread or crackers, etc. Also bring something to drink. As the students arrive, let them snack. Encourage them to taste some of each kind of bread and compare the flavors.

DISCOVERY RALLY

Gather the students together in a large group.

WHAT'S THE GOOD WORD?

Choose a student to read the Scripture for the day.

THE CHALLENGE

Ask: **Which bread was your favorite? Which was your least favorite?** Say: **All over the world, people eat more bread than any other food. Bread is sometimes called "the staff of life," meaning that most people use it to receive life and health through its nourishment. But just as our bodies depend on food to be healthy physically, so our spirits depend on Jesus to be healthy spiritually. In this way, Jesus is truly the Bread of our lives.**

Tell the students that in their Discovery Centers today they will find out more about Jesus as Lord. He has the authority to feed and nourish our spirits.

PRAYER

DISCOVERY CENTERS

1. BREAD OF LIFE MOSAIC

DO: Give each student a piece of construction paper and a marker. Ask them to turn the papers so that the long sides form the top and bottom. They write "The Bread of Life—John 6:35" across the bottom of the paper. Then they glue croutons onto the paper to form the word JESUS.

MATERIALS
construction paper, plain croutons, glue, markers

DISCUSS: Ask: **Why did Jesus called himself the Bread of Life? How does he feed our spirits?** Say: **Just as food helps us grow physically, Jesus' teachings help us grow in our spirits and in our minds. Food gives us strength and energy. Jesus, living in us through his Holy Spirit, gives us strength**

and energy. Encourage students to tell about a time when they or someone they knew needed Jesus' strength and energy. Ask: **How can we get this spiritual bread?** (We can read Jesus' teachings. We can accept Jesus as Savior and Lord. We can pray. We can live our lives by following Jesus.)

2. VITAMIN L

DO: Let each student get a handful of play dough to put on a paper plate. Ask students to form it into an oval shape that looks like a huge vitamin. Pour some alphabet cereal or pasta onto some extra paper plates, and let each student find letters that spell "Vitamin L." Students gently press these letters into their play dough vitamins and leave them to dry. Let students examine the bread package to find out what vitamins are in the bread. Then let students clean their hands with the wipes and eat a piece of bread.

MATERIALS

a variety of colors of play dough, paper plate alphabet-shaped dry cereal or pasta, a loaf bread in its package, hand wipes, a Bible

DISCUSS: Ask: **Why do food packages list the vitamins in the food? What vitamins does bread have in it? Name some other vitamins. What does vitamin C do for you? What does vitamin A do?** Say: **Vitamin L is a spiritual vitamin—LOVE. It's a vitamin everyone needs. Why? The best source of vitamin L (Love) is Jesus. Where can we find out about Jesus' love?** Ask someone to read John 10:27-29. Say: **That's how much Jesus loves you.** Ask someone to read 2 Peter 1:3. Say: **That's how much Jesus loves you.** Ask: **Name some other things that show how much Jesus loves you.**

3. WISE TEACHINGS

MATERIALS
beginnings and endings cards from pages 57–60, two different colors of paper, scissors, a Bible

DO: Before class, copy the beginnings cards onto one color of paper and cut them out. Copy the endings cards onto a different color of paper and cut them out. Keep beginning cards in one stack, numbered one through twenty. Keep ending cards in another stack, also numbered one through twenty. Select the number of cards you need from the beginnings stack so that each student will get one card. Begin at number one. Do the same with the endings stack. Now mix the beginnings cards up and deal them out to the students. Then mix the endings cards up and deal them to the students. Choose one student to begin play. This student reads the beginning written on his first card, followed by the ending on his other card. In all likelihood, they will not match. The other students try to decide if the beginning matches the ending, or if they think the ending card they hold is the one that completes that beginning. If a student thinks she has the ending, she challenges the reader by saying, "I have the real bread." Then the reader reads the beginning again, and the challenger reads the ending. To find out if this is the correct ending, students may look up the Scripture in the Bible. Then the student to the reader's left reads his beginning and ending. If you have time, you may play another round by choosing new cards from the stacks and repeating the game process.

DISCUSS: Feel free to allow discussion on some of these teachings. Ask: **If Jesus is the Bread of Life, then what does that say about his teachings? Are these teachings true? How could they feed your spirit? Have you heard any of these teachings before? If so, which ones? Are any of these teachings new to you? If so, which ones? When you eat, does the food nourish your body if you simply chew it but don't swallow? When you hear Jesus' teachings, does it do you any good to simply listen but not obey? Why or why not?**

If you have time to review, gather as a large group and discuss your young discoverers' findings. Ask the following questions:

- **What did Jesus mean when he said, "I am the Bread of Life"?**
- **How does Jesus feed our spirits?**
- **How can we find out about Jesus' love?**
- **How much does Jesus love us?**
- **What's important about Jesus' teachings?**
- **What does it mean when we ask Jesus to be our Lord?**

Review the Scripture for today.

Pray, thanking God for making Jesus our Lord and our Bread of Life. Ask God to keep feeding our spirits through Jesus.

Jesus' Wise Teachings:
Beginnings

1
"Don't hide your light under a basket, but…"
Matthew 5:15

2
"If you are ordered to court and your shirt is taken from you…"
Matthew 5:40

3
"If a soldier demands that you carry his gear for a mile…"
Matthew 5:41

4
"Give to those who ask, and…"
Matthew 5:42

5
"Love your enemies, and"
Matthew 5:44

6
"If you are slapped on the right cheek…"
Matthew 5:39

7
"When you give to someone,
Matthew 6:3

8
"When you pray…"
Matthew 6:7

9
"If you forgive those who sin against you…"
Matthew 6:14

10
"Wherever your treasure is…"
Matthew 6:21

Jesus' Wise Teachings:
More Beginnings

11

"Whatever measure you use in judging others..."
Matthew 7:2

12

"Keep on looking, and..."
Matthew 7:7

13

"Don't worry about tomorrow, for..."
Matthew 6:34

14

"Come to me, all of you who are weary and carry heavy burdens, and..."
Matthew 11:28

15

"If you give up your life for me..."
Matthew 16:25

16

"Let the children come to me. Don't stop them. For..."
Matthew 19:14

17

"Honor your father and..."
Matthew 19:19

18

"Whoever wants to be a leader among you must be your servant, and..."
Matthew 20:26, 27

19

"Give to Caesar what belongs to him. But. . .
Matthew 22:21

20

"When you pray..."
Matthew 6:6

Jesus' Wise Teachings:
Endings

1 "...put it on a stand and let it shine for all."	**2** "...give your coat, too."
3 "...carry it two miles."	**4** "...don't turn away from those who borrow."
5 "...pray for those who persecute you."	**6** "...turn the other, too."
7 "...don't tell your left hand what your right hand is doing."	**8** "...don't babble on and on."
9 "...your heavenly Father will forgive you."	**10** "...there your heart and thoughts will also be."

Jesus' Wise Teachings:
More Endings

11
"...it will be used to measure how you are judged."

12
"...you will find."

13
"...tomorrow will bring its own worries."

14
"...I will give you rest."

15
"...you will find true life."

16
"...the Kingdom of Heaven belongs to such as these."

17
"...mother."

18
"...whoever wants to be first must become your slave."

19
"...everything that belongs to God must be given to God."

20
"...go away by yourself, shut the door behind you."

The Servant Lord

scripture

"Christ himself was like God in everything. He was equal with God. But he did not think that being equal with God was something to be held on to. He gave up his place with God and made himself nothing. He was born to be a man and became like a servant." Philippians 2:6, 7, ICB

Goal

Learn that Jesus the Lord served those over whom he had authority.

INTRODUCTION

Before this session, make a "Job Jar." On strips of paper, write tasks that students can do to help with the upkeep of your classroom. These might be: wash tables, clean windows, straighten cabinets or shelves, sweep floor, dust, empty the trash, collect materials for today's activities (be specific), etc. Provide the broom, dust cloths, and any other equipment needed to complete these tasks. Fold the paper strips and place them in a wide mouthed jar or bowl. Also ask someone from your church whom the students would identify as a leader to come in and help the students clean. (In order to drive home the point of this session, this person must really work and not simply watch or supervise.) As students arrive, they draw one of the strips of paper from the job jar, read it, and do what it says. They may work individually or in pairs. Join them yourself in helping to clean the room. If you anticipate that some will finish their tasks early, you may provide something to drink and a snack to eat when they finish.

DISCOVERY RALLY

Gather the students together in a large group.

WHAT'S THE GOOD WORD?

Choose a student to read the Scripture for the day.

THE CHALLENGE

Point out that the jobs the students did earlier were ways of serving each other, serving you the teacher, and serving your church. Say: **Some people would be surprised that a leader like** (the leader from your church who helped) **would help clean up and serve.** Then tell them this true incident: There was a missionary in Kenya, Africa who was the head of a Bible college. He had an office and held meetings and even taught some classes. One day, there was a lot of clean-up work that needed to be done at the college, so this missionary leader took a bucket and some cleaning supplies and began to clean the toilets. The students were shocked. "You can't clean the toilets," they said. "You are the head of the college!" Ask: **What was this leader showing the students by his actions? What was our own leader showing us by his actions?** Say: **The Lord Jesus, the greatest leader of all became a servant.**

Tell the students that in their Discovery Centers today they will find out more about how the Lord of all the universe served people.

PRAYER

DISCOVERY CENTERS

1. SPONGE PRINT MURAL

DO: Spread the butcher paper on the floor or attach to a wall. Spread newspapers around the floor in the work area. Give each student a large sponge and assign him to a spot on the butcher paper. Pour enough of the same color of paint in each plate to cover the bottom of the plate. Tell students to gently press a sponge into the paint. The first student on the left of the mural will paint a large "S" by pressing the sponge onto the paper repeatedly to make an "S" shape. The student to her right paints an "E." Each student in line continues with letters to spell SERVANT LORD. If you don't have enough students in the first group, your second group can finish the words.

MATERIALS

a six-foot length of butcher paper, heavy paper plates or disposable aluminum pie pans, washable liquid paint, old newspapers, several large and small sponges, water for clean-up, non-permanent markers, servant cards copied and cut out from page 66

Once the students have finished printing their letters, they serve by cleaning up and preparing new pans of paint, a different color, for the next group. (If your second group will finish the original words, keep one pan with the first color of paint.)

In your second group, some students will finish printing any large letters on the mural, while the others will use the smaller sponges to print a border around the left hand side of each letter with the second color of paint. Then they clean up. If any letters don't yet have a border, leave one pan of paint for finishing this in the third group.

In your third group, students may finish printing a border for any letters that need it. Other students choose a servant card. With a marker, they copy the incidents listed on the cards onto the mural at random in the spaces around the top, bottom and sides of the large printed letters.

DISCUSS: Say: **The Lord Jesus, the greatest ruler of all became a servant. Why? What did Jesus do to prove that he was a servant? How can a person be a servant and a leader at the same time? Does it make you respect a**

leader more, or less, when you see the leader do something that a servant would normally do? Why?

2. FOOTPRINTS

MATERIALS
a roll of aluminum foil, large construction paper, stapler and staples, a Bible

DO: Give each student two pieces of aluminum foil about two to four inches longer than their shoes. Working in pairs, let the students help each other mold the foil around the soles of each shoe so that the shape and pattern of the sole are molded clearly into the foil. Then students take the foil off of the shoe, being careful to preserve the shape. Give each student a piece of construction paper. Let them staple the top edge of both footprints to the paper so they can be displayed.

DISCUSS: Ask someone to read John 13:3-5 and 12-15. Ask: **What was Jesus showing us? Why? What are some other things Jesus did that served others? Do you think there were any jobs that Jesus would not do? Why or why not? If Jesus is a servant, how can he also be Lord?**

3. SERVANTS WHO BECAME LEADERS

MATERIALS
a copy of the Servants and Leaders page (pages 67-69), scissors, a variety of colors of play dough, a piece of paper and a pen

DO: Cut apart the descriptions of the Servant-Leaders. Fold each description in half to hide its contents, and give one to each student. Tell the students to read secretly the description they have and then sculpt an object that represents that leader's story. Write down the servant-leaders' names on a piece of paper or chalk board so everyone can see the possible answers. Then let the students guess which leader each sculpted object represents. The sculptor may give verbal clues if necessary. You may let students work in pairs if you wish. The following are some suggestions you can make to help students if they can't think of an object to sculpt.

Joseph: pyramid, colorful coat, moon, stars
David: harp, sheep, crown

King Saul: donkey, baggage, crown

Moses: staff, sheep, burning bush

Joshua: tent, sword, shield

Daniel: lion, vegetables, water

Gideon: wheat, angel, horn, torch

Esther: crown, scepter

Samuel: bed, lamp, robe

Peter: fish, lake, boat

DISCUSS: Point out that each of these leaders began their lives by being servants. Ask: **What did each of these leaders learn by first being a servant?** Then ask someone to read Philippians 2:5-7. Ask: **Who was Jesus before he became a servant? Why did he become a servant? What do you think Jesus learned by being a servant?** Ask someone to read Hebrews 2:18. Then read Philippians 2:8-11. Ask: **After being a servant, what position did Jesus take? What is it that God wants us to confess about Jesus?**

DISCOVERERS' DEBRIEFING

If you have time to review, gather as a large group and discuss your young discoverers' findings. Since only one group got to list some of Jesus' jobs on the mural, you may want to gather around the Servant Lord mural and review the descriptions of what Jesus did as a servant. Then ask the following questions:

- **What is the most interesting thing you discovered today?**
- **What did you learn today that you did not know before?**
- **How can someone be a servant and a leader at the same time?**
- **What did Jesus do to show that he was a servant?**
- **What position does Jesus have now?**
- **What does God want us to confess about Jesus?**

Review the Scripture for today.

Pray, thanking God for sending Jesus to be a servant who experienced life as a human being. Praise Jesus and confess that he is Lord.

Servant Cards

Jesus turned water into wine for a wedding. John 2:1-11	Jesus healed a blind beggar. John 9:1-9
Jesus touched and healed a man who had leprosy. Luke 5:12-14	Jesus brought a widow's only son back to life. Luke 7:11-15
Jesus calmed a storm when his disciples were scared. Luke 8:22-25	Jesus went to help his friends who were having a hard time sailing across the lake. Matthew 14:22-33
Jesus defended a woman who was being criticized. Matthew 26:6-13	Jesus fed 5,000 hungry people. John 6:1-13
Jesus washed his disciples' feet. John 13:1-17	Jesus healed a man with a deformed right hand. Luke 6:6-10
Jesus ate with tax collectors, who were thought to be worthless people. Luke 5:27-32	Jesus held and blessed little children. Luke 18:15-17
Jesus paid taxes. Matthew 17:24-27	Jesus chose friends who were common people. Mark 3:13-19

Servants and Leaders

These are people who started their lives being servants, but ended up being leaders. Choose one of them, read that person's story, then using clay, make a clue about the person you've chosen. Your friends will guess who your secret servant-leader is.

JOSEPH   Genesis 37-41

I was next to the youngest of 12 sons. My father gave me a colorful coat. One night I dreamed that 11 stars were bowing to me. But then I was taken as a slave to Egypt. I was thrown into prison, even though I hadn't done wrong. After many years, I was set free. The king of Egypt put me in charge of the whole land!

DAVID   1 Samuel 16-2 Samuel 5

I was a shepherd when I was a boy. I had seven older brothers. I loved to play the harp, and I was very good at throwing rocks with my slingshot. I got a good job playing harp for the king. But the king didn't like me, so I had to run from him. I became a leader of a group of fighters. Then after the king died, I became king!

SAUL   1 Samuel 9, 10

I was the least important person in my family. And my family was from the least important family group in Israel. One day I was out looking for my father's lost donkeys when a prophet told me that I would one day be king. It was hard to believe. Even when the people came to make me king, I was so shy that I hid behind some baggage. But they brought me out, and I did become king!

MOSES   Exodus 2-13

Although I grew up in a palace in Egypt, I was not truly a member of the royal family. One day I killed a man who was attacking one of my own people. Then I had to run away. I ended up herding sheep. One day I saw a bush that was on fire, but it did not burn up. God spoke to me from the bush and told me that I would lead his people out of Egypt. And that's just what I did. I became a famous leader!

JOSHUA
Exodus 24:13-33:11; Numbers 27

I was Moses' helper. I listened to him, followed him, and served him. When Moses went into the Meeting Tent to spend time with God, I went too. I would stay in the tent for a long time. Before Moses died, he told me that I would become the leader of God's people. And that's just what happened. I led them into the land that God had promised to give them. We had to fight to take the land, so I became a leader in battle.

DANIEL
Daniel 1-6

As a young man, I was taken captive by enemy soldiers. They took me to a country far away. There I was chosen with some of my friends to be trained to serve the king. We were to eat special food from the king's table. But I asked for vegetables and water instead. As it turned out, my friends and I were chosen to serve the king. We had many adventures. I was even thrown into a lion's den for refusing to pray to the king. But God protected me, and I ended up being one of the most important leaders in the land.

GIDEON
Judges 6, 7

I was a young man from the weakest family group of Israel. One day I was at work, separating seeds from the harvested wheat, when an angel came to me. He called me a mighty warrior. He said God had chosen me. God told me just what to do, and I obeyed. I ended up leading a group of men into a battle that we won simply by blowing horns and waving torches in the air! Then I kept leading God's people.

ESTHER
Esther 2-5

I was an orphan. My older cousin took care of me. The king of our land was looking for a new queen. I was taken to the palace along with lots of other young women who were hoping to become the new queen. But the king liked me best of all, so I became the queen of the whole land! Even though no one could go to see the king unless he asked them to come, I went to see him to ask him to save God's people. The king loved me enough to hold his scepter out to me. I realized that God had made me queen so that I could help save his people.

SAMUEL   1 Samuel 2, 3

I was just a little boy when I started serving in the worship house with the old priest Eli. Every year my mother would bring me a new robe to wear. One night I went to bed before the lamp had gone out. While I was lying there, I heard a voice call me. I thought it was Eli. But when I ran to him, he told me he had not called. At last I realized that God was calling my name. I told God that I was listening, and he told me a message that I later gave Eli. God spoke to me often, and when I grew up, I became a leader of God's people, giving them God's messages.

PETER   Matthew 4:18-20; Acts 2:14-41

I used to go fishing with my brother. Fishing became our job, and we worked with a group of fishermen. Then one day, Jesus asked us to follow him. So we did. Jesus taught us about God's kingdom and showed us the way to live. He taught us how to teach and help others. After Jesus went back to heaven, I became a leader in the church.

The Lord's Servants

scripture

"Jesus replied, 'You must love the Lord your God with all your heart, all your soul, and all your mind. This is the first and greatest commandment.'"
Matthew 22:37, 38, NLT

Goal

Learn that we respond to Jesus' lordship by loving and serving him.

INTRODUCTION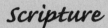

As students arrive, give each one a pencil and a copy of the Up and Down Cipher (page 75). Ask them to follow the directions to practice writing their names in this code. As they continue to follow the directions, they can decode a message that tells what Jesus said was the most important thing to do. You should practice the code ahead of time so that you can help them if necessary. Children who quickly figure out the code can help others as they arrive.

DISCOVERY RALLY

Gather the students together in a large group.

WHAT'S THE GOOD WORD?

Choose a student to read the Scripture for the day.

THE CHALLENGE

Ask the students if the Scripture for the day sounded familiar. Ask them to tell you what their coded message said. Then ask them to name some positions of leadership (parent, teacher, governor, mayor, king, president, etc.). Ask: **What does it take to be a leader? What does it take to be a king? What does it take to be a president?** Students may answer in a variety of ways. Lead them to understand that in order to be a leader, a person must be a follower or a servant. Ask: **What are Jesus' followers called?** (Christians, disciples, servants of the Lord, the church)

Tell the students that in their Discovery Centers today they will find out what we become when we choose Jesus as our Lord.

PRAYER

DISCOVERY CENTERS

1. HEART SUN-CATCHER

DO: Cover a work surface with an old towel. Lay newspaper on top of the towel. Give each student two 12" lengths of wax paper. Students place one of their sheets of wax paper over the heart pattern page and trace over the heart shapes with a permanent marker. Then they sharpen crayons over the hearts, letting the crayon shavings fall on top of the hearts. They lay the second piece of wax paper on top. Now they gently iron over this top layer so that the colored shavings melt. They cut out the heart

MATERIALS

several copies of the heart patterns on page 76, permanent markers, wax paper, crayons, a crayon (or pencil) sharpener, old newspaper, an old towel, an iron, scissors, a hole puncher, colorful yarn shapes, punch a hole in the top and bottom center of each heart, and then tie the hearts together with yarn, leaving a length at the top so they can hang this sun-catcher in a window at home. On the top heart, they write "Love." On the middle heart, they write, "the Lord." On the bottom heart, they write, "with all your heart."

DISCUSS: As the students work, ask: **Do you have to love a president in order for him to be your president? Do you have to love a king in order for him to be your king? Why does Jesus say that the most important thing in God's kingdom is to love the Lord with all your heart, soul, and mind?** (We have no choice but to live under most of these earthly rulers. We can vote for some of our leaders, but if someone is elected and we didn't vote for him or her, we are under their leadership anyway. We have no choice. But Jesus allows each of us to choose whether or not to follow him. We don't have to let him be Lord of our lives, even though he's the Lord of heaven and earth. He wants us to follow him not because we have to, but because we love him and choose to follow him.) Ask: **How would someone show love for the Lord?**

2. A TEMPLE FIGURE

MATERIALS
paper, crayons or watercolor markers, a Bible

DO: Give each student a piece of paper and a crayon or marker. Ask the students to follow your directions as you guide them to make a drawing. Give the following instructions:

• Draw a capital T about as tall as your hand in the center of your paper.
  The top bar of the T forms the arms of your figure.
• Draw a capital P, about half as tall as the T, standing in the center of the top bar of the T. This makes the neck and head of your figure.
• Draw two capital L's as legs attached to the bottom of the T.
• Draw two small capital E's, one at each end of the bar of the T to form hands.

- Draw a small capital M somewhere on the head of the figure to form the hair.
- Across the top of the page, draw six blanks. The letters that form this figure spell a word. The word starts with a T, so write T in the first blank. Try to fill in the other blanks. One letter in the figure will not be used.

DISCUSS: Encourage the students to guess what the second letter might be, then the third and so on, giving hints, until someone figures out what the word is. Ask: **What is a temple?** (It's a building used for worship.) Ask someone to read 1 Corinthians 3:16. Ask students to write across the bottom of their papers: "I am a temple. 1 Corinthians 3:16." Ask: **If a temple was made for worship, and you are a temple, what were you made for?** (We were made to worship.) Ask someone to tell what the Scripture for today is. Say: **Loving the Lord with all your heart, soul, and mind is worship. If we are temples, we can choose what to allow into our temples. Name some things that people "love." Are any of these things Lord? Who is Lord? It only makes sense to worship the greatest, the Lord.**

If you have time, ask the students to draw eyes, nose and mouth in the loop of the P, and to color clothes on their figures if they want. They can also try making a figure out of the letters of their names.

3. THE SERVANT'S TRAY

MATERIALS
a tray, paper cups, a Bible

DO: Mark a starting point and an ending point for a path across your room, or down a hall, or outdoors. Ask the students to line up. Give the tray to the first student. Place two paper cups upside down on the tray, and place a third cup on top of the first two to make a pyramid. Ask the student to carry the tray, balanced on one hand, down the path and back. The student tries to complete the path with the pyramid of cups intact. He then hands the tray to the next student in line. This student walks the path too. When all students have walked the path, add enough cups to make a taller pyramid. Anytime the cups fall, the tray automatically goes to the next person in line. See who can carry the tallest pyramid of cups successfully.

DISCUSS: Ask: **What kind of servant might carry a tray?** Then ask someone to read James 1:1. Ask: **What does James call himself? Why? What does a servant do?** Say: **When we accept Jesus as our Lord, we become his servants. How can we serve Jesus?** Remind the students of the Scripture for today. Ask: **What is the most important thing the Lord wants his servants to do? Why do people love the Lord?** Read 1 John 4:19. Ask: **How do we know Jesus loves us?** Read Ephesians 3:16-19. Ask: **How great is the Lord's love for us?** Say: **As we get to know Jesus better, we realize all that he does for us because of his love, and the more we love him.** Ask: **How can we show our love for the Lord?**

DISCOVERERS' DEBRIEFING

If you have time to review, gather as a large group and discuss your young discoverers' findings. Ask the following questions:

• **What is the most interesting thing you discovered today?**
• **What did you learn today that you did not know before?**
• **If Jesus is our Lord, what does that make us?**
• **What did Jesus say is the most important thing for us to do?**
• **What does it mean for us to be temples for the Lord?**
• **What does it mean for us to be servants of the Lord?**
• **How can we show our love for the Lord?**

Review the Scripture for today.

Pray, asking God to help us love the Lord with all our hearts, souls, and minds. Thank him for choosing us to be temples for worshiping and loving him. Thank him for first loving us and being our Lord.

Up and Down Cipher

Here's how to write a message in cipher. Let's say that our message is:

Jesus is Lord

1. Write the message in all capital letters: **JESUS IS LORD**

2. Take out all the spaces. If there are commas and periods, take those out too:

JESUSISLORD

3. Count the number of letters in the message. This message has 11 letters.

4. You must have an even number of letters, so add one extra letter at the end, any letter you want. It's called a "null." **JESUSISLORDM**

5. Now write the letters in order, but on two lines. The first letter goes on the top line. The second letter goes on the second line, like this:

J S S S O D
E U I L R M

6. Write the letters of the top line and then the letters of the bottom line.

JSSSODEUILRM

7. Divide the letters into groups to look like words.

JSSSO DE UIL RM

To decode a message like this, work backward. Take out all the spaces between letters. Divide the number of letters in half. Write the first half of the letters on one line with spaces between the letters. On the second line, write the second half of the letters under the spaces on the first line. Then put the lower letters into the spaces in the first line. Then figure out where to put the spaces between the words.

Now that you know how the code works, decode this message:

LVTE OD IHLY UHATO EHLR WTAL ORERX

Heart Patterns

Trusting in the Lord

Scripture

"Trust in the Lord with all your heart; do not depend on your own understanding." Proverbs 3:5, NLT

Goal

Learn that accepting Jesus as Lord means trusting him.

INTRODUCTION

As students arrive, give each one a pencil and a copy of the Heart Squares (page 82). As they finish finding the hidden word, encourage them to try hiding their own names in heart squares that they design.

DISCOVERY RALLY

Gather the students together in a large group.

WHAT'S THE GOOD WORD?

Choose a student to read the Scripture for the day.

THE CHALLENGE

Note: This activity will require you to catch the full weight of students as they

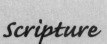

gently fall backward. If you are not strong enough to do this, ask a stronger person to join your group to help with this challenge. Also ask this person to help in Group 3 today.

Ask: **What word did you discover in your heart squares? What does it mean to trust?** Tell the students that you (or your helper) is very good at catching things. Ask the students if they trust you. Ask a student who has said yes to stand in front of you or your helper. The student's back should be toward you. Tell the student to keep his arms to his side, legs stiff and straight, and fall backwards. You (or your helper) will catch the student. As he falls backwards, catch him as you've promised. Point out that this is trust. Say: **It's easy for us to say we trust. But real trust shows up in what we do. It's easy to say that Jesus is our Lord. But if he is really our Lord, we have to trust him enough to let him control our lives.**

Tell the students that in their Discovery Centers today they will find out more about how trust is an important part of accepting Jesus as Lord.

PRAYER

DISCOVERY CENTERS

1. WHO WEARS THE CROWN?

MATERIALS
a crown made by cutting a 2" section around the middle of an empty plastic gallon milk or water jug

DO: Ask the students to sit in a circle. Choose one of them to stand in the center with eyes closed. The other students start passing the crown around the circle. When you say STOP, the student holding the crown places it on her head and asks, disguising her voice as much as possible, "Who wears the crown?" The student in the center tries to guess who's speaking. If the guess is correct, the guesser trades places with the student wearing the crown, and the game

starts again. If the guess is incorrect, the crown continues around the circle for another round.

DISCUSS: Stop the game after it has been going for awhile so that you can have a discussion. Ask: **Who is the King of Kings and the Lord of Lords? How does he become the Lord of your life? When we ask Jesus to be Lord of our lives, we are putting him in charge. We might say that Jesus wears the crown. Why does the Lord want you to trust him? Is it always easy to trust the Lord? Why or why not? Can Jesus really be your Lord if you don't trust him?**

2. THE PUZZLE

MATERIALS
markers, 1/4 of a piece of poster board for each student, scissors

DO: Give each student 1/4 of a piece of poster board. Ask the students to write, "Trust in the Lord" on their posters. Then ask them to cut the posters into eight large jigsaw puzzle pieces and write their name on the back of each piece. Now they mix their puzzle pieces up and pass them to the student on their left. Students put together their neighbor's puzzle. Keep passing the puzzles and working them until the pieces come back to their original owner.

DISCUSS: From your own puzzle or one of the student's puzzles, hold up one piece. Say: **Our lives are a little bit like a puzzle piece. Sometimes it's hard to figure out where and how we are supposed to fit into this world. But who knows where and how we fit? The Lord does. He is in charge, and he created each of us for a purpose. We may not know what the purpose is, but he does. So we trust him with our lives. We put ourselves into his hands. Point to the puzzle piece in your hand. We say, "Put me where YOU want me to be, Lord."** Now work the puzzle. Say: **Then the Lord links us with others and makes life work the way he created it to work.** Ask: **How can you show that you trust the Lord with your life?**

3. THE TRUSTWORTHY ONE

MATERIALS

a sturdy chair, a paper grocery bag, a Bible

DO: Open the grocery bag and stand it upside down in front of your students. Set the chair beside it. Ask one student: **Which of these would you trust to hold your weight if you stood on it?** After the student answers, say: **Prove it.** The student stands on the chair or bag, whichever he answered. Say: **Trust is not just something you believe, think, or say. It's something you do.** Then let the students take turns falling backward into your (or your helper's) arms as described in the Discovery Rally challenge.

DISCUSS: Ask: **Why do you trust me** (or the helper)**? Am I trustworthy? If I didn't catch the person before you, would you trust me to catch you? If I tell you I'll do something and I keep my promise, you know you can trust me. I am trustworthy. How do you know you can trust the Lord? If you don't trust him, can he really be your Lord?** Ask someone to read Jeremiah 17:5-8. Ask: **How does Jeremiah describe a person who doesn't trust in the Lord? How does he describe a person who trusts in the Lord? How does a person show that they trust the Lord?**

DISCOVERERS' DEBRIEFING

Discoverers' Debriefing

If you have time to review, gather as a large group and discuss your young discoverers' findings. Ask the following questions:

- **What is the most interesting thing you discovered today?**
- **What did you learn today that you did not know before?**
- **What does it mean to trust the Lord?**
- **How did Jeremiah describe people who don't trust in the Lord? How did he describe people who do trust in the Lord?**
- **Why is the Lord trustworthy?**
- **Can Jesus be our Lord if we don't trust him? Why or why not?**

Review the Scripture for today.

Pray, thanking the Lord for keeping his promises and being trustworthy. Ask him to help you trust him more.

Heart Squares

In each section, there are squares with hearts in them. In each section, draw a line through the squares that have hearts, connecting them. Then read the word you've spelled.

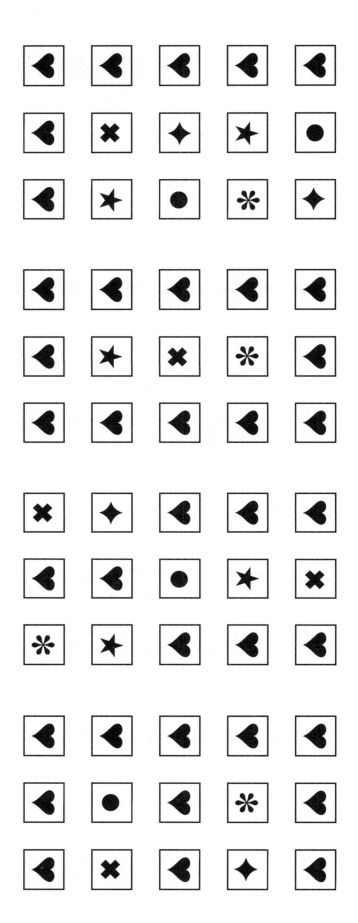

Obeying the Lord

Scripture

"Not everyone who says to me, 'Lord, Lord,' will enter the kingdom of heaven, but only he who does the will of my Father who is in heaven." Matthew 7:21, NIV

Goal

Learn that accepting Jesus as Lord means obeying him.

INTRODUCTION

When the first few students arrive, choose one of them to be the first leader for the game "Land, Sea, Air." Ask them to choose hand motions that they will use to represent the sea, the land, and the air. (If they need help, suggest rowing for the sea, pounding fists together for land, flying for air.) The leader then calls out, "Land, sea, air, land, sea, air" as the others do the appropriate motions. Then the leader calls out any type of transportation. The others must do the motions that show what that transportation travels on. Continue in this way for a few minutes. Then let the leader choose a new leader to take his place. As children arrive, explain the game, and let them join in.

DISCOVERY RALLY

Gather the students together in a large group.

WHAT'S THE GOOD WORD?

Choose a student to read the Scripture for the day.

THE CHALLENGE

Point out that in order to play the game "Land, Sea, Air," everyone had to know and follow the rules. Ask the students to tell you what sports they play and to tell you one rule for that sport. Ask: **What happens if the team you're playing against doesn't follow the rules?** Say: **You are free to play and have a good game as long as everyone follows the rules. The game doesn't work right unless everyone obeys.** Tell the students about a pilot who said, "We pilots are free to fly if we obey the laws of flying every moment." Ask: **Why do pilots have to obey the laws of flying?** Say: **Flying doesn't work unless pilots obey the rules.**

Tell your students that in their Discovery Centers today they will find out how important it is to obey Jesus if we truly want him to be our Lord.

PRAYER

DISCOVERY CENTERS

1. ALLERGIC TO SIN

DO: Give each student a card. Tell the students that these are common things that cause allergies in people. Without showing the card to anyone, each student in turn gives up to three clues about what's on the card. The others guess what it is. If they don't guess after three clues, the student tells them what it is.

> **MATERIALS**
>
> index cards on which you've written the following words, one item per card: dust, cats, perfume, poison ivy, bee stings, milk, eggs, wheat, trees, soap, medicines, peanuts

DISCUSS: Ask the students if any of them have allergies. If so, let them tell what they are allergic to and how the allergy affects them. Tell them that allergies can cause a runny nose, sneezing, itchy eyes, itchy skin, swelling and redness of skin, difficulty in breathing or asthma, and upset stomach. Say: **There is one thing that everyone in the world is allergic to: sin. Jesus showed us how life works. We were built to obey the laws of God's Kingdom. If what we want to do doesn't fit into God's Kingdom, then it's wrong to do it. If we do wrong, we sin, and life doesn't work. Things go wrong. It's like being allergic to sin. So when we ask Jesus to be our Lord, we're saying that we want to obey the ways of God's Kingdom like Jesus did.** If you have time, ask your students to name some things that people their age might do that we would call sin. Ask: **What are some of the bad things that happen when people speak rudely or cheat or steal?** Try to steer the discussion to the injustice done to others as well as the penalties of getting caught.

2. A WORD CHAIN

MATERIALS
copies of the Word Chain (page 88),
a Bible, pencils

DO: Give each student a pencil and a copy of the Word Chain page. Ask one of the students to read James 1:22, the verse written at the top of the page. Then tell the students to use the underlined words in the verse to fill in the word chains. The last letter of most words in the chain is the first letter of the following word in the chain.

DISCUSS: Ask: **Why are you fooling yourself if you only listen to God's teaching and do nothing?** Ask someone to read Matthew 7:21, the Scripture for today. Ask: **What did Jesus mean when he said that? How can someone call Jesus "Lord" and not do God's will?** Ask someone to read Matthew 15:8, 9. Ask: **What were the people doing that was wrong?** Then ask: **Why does Jesus want to be our Lord? Why does he want to tell us how to think and act? Why should we obey him?** Say: **Jesus knows how life works. He doesn't want us to live worried, fearful, sad, miserable lives. So he shows us how to live. When we ask Jesus to be our Lord, we are choosing to trust and obey him.** Ask someone to read Galatians 5:19-23 to find the results of disobeying and obeying God.

3. OBEY TO PLAY

MATERIALS
coins, a Bible

DO: Ask each student to pair up with a partner. Tell your students that they will be doing some stunts together, but in order to accomplish the stunts they will have to listen. Not only will they have to listen, but they will also have to do exactly what they're told. In other words, they'll have to obey your directions. Give them the following directions.

- Stand with your elbows bent. Touch the tips of your index fingers together. Your partner should now try to pull your fingers apart. Now trade places so your partner can do the stunt.

- Stand with your feet and back against a wall. Your partner should set a coin on the floor in front of your feet. Try to pick the coin up without bending your knees or moving your feet at all. Now trade places with your partner.

- Stand with your arms stretched out in front of you. Place one fist on top of the other. Try to keep your fists in this position. Your partner should try to separate your fists by using only his or her index fingers and quickly hitting the back of each fist at the same time, pushing sideways. Trade places with your partner.

- With your arm out to the side, bend your forearm up and place your hand on top of your head. Keep your elbow up. Your partner tries to lift your hand off of your head. Trade places with your partner.

After the stunts, ask students to sit down.

DISCUSS: Ask: **Have you ever done these stunts before? Do you think you might be able to teach these stunts to a friend or family member later? What if you had only listened to my instructions, but didn't do what I said to do?** Ask someone to read James 1:22. Ask: **Why would we be fooling or deceiving ourselves if we only read about the Lord but never do what he teaches? Can we really call Jesus our Lord if we never do what he says? Why or why not? Just as we never experience the fun of the stunts if we don't obey the directions, so we never experience how great life can be if we don't obey Jesus our Lord.**

DISCOVERERS' DEBRIEFING

Discoverers' Debriefing Debriefing

If you have time to review, gather as a large group and discuss your young discoverers' findings. Ask the following questions:

- **What is the most interesting thing you discovered today?**
- **What did you learn today that you did not know before?**
- **Why is it important to obey the Lord?**
- **What do we mean by saying we're allergic to sin?**
- **Why are you fooling yourself if you only listen to God's teaching but do nothing?**
- **Why should we obey Jesus?**

Review the Scripture for today.

Pray, thanking God for sending Jesus to show us how to live. Ask him to help us obey.

A Word Chain

Use the underlined words in the Scripture to fill in the chains. The last letter of most words is the first letter of the next word.

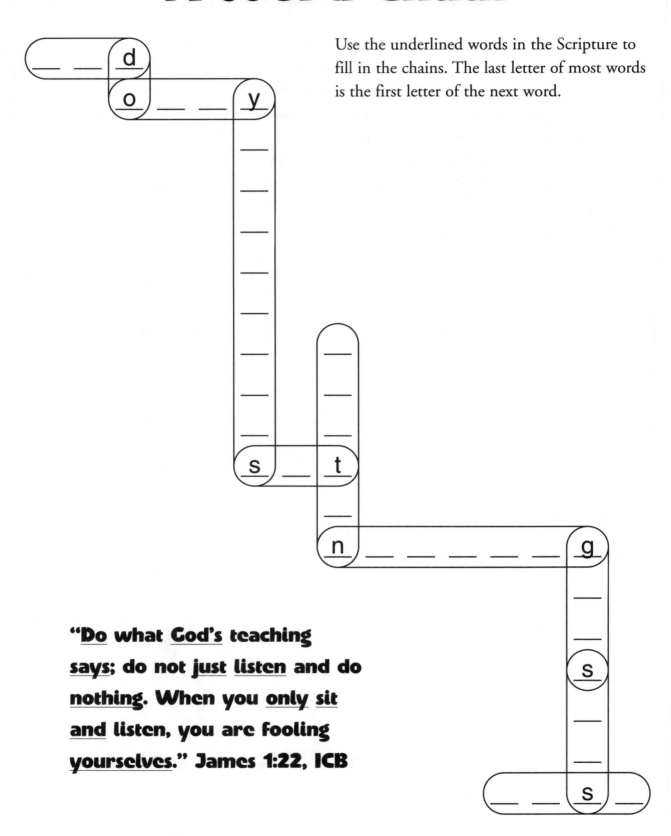

__ __ d

o __ __ y

s __ t

n __ __ __ __ __ g

s

s __ __

"**Do** what **God's** teaching **says**; do not just **listen** and do **nothing**. When you **only** **sit** **and** listen, you are fooling **yourselves**." James 1:22, ICB

Every Knee Shall Bow

Scripture

"At the name of Jesus every knee will bow, in heaven and on earth and under the earth, and every tongue will confess that Jesus Christ is Lord."
Philippians 2:10, 11, NLT

Goal

Learn that God wants everyone in the world to acknowledge that Jesus is Lord.

INTRODUCTION

As students arrive, give each one a pencil and a copy of Fact or Opinion? (page 93). Ask them to write F by each statement that is a fact and O by each statement that is an opinion. You may need to help them, reminding them that an opinion is something that may be true for one person, but not true for another. A fact is right all the time, and if another person disagreed with it, they would be wrong. For example, 2 + 2 = 4. That's a fact, even if someone disagreed with it. But if someone said, "Math is hard," that's an opinion. For someone else, math might be easy.

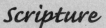

DISCOVERY RALLY

Discovery Rally
Rally

Gather the students together in a large group.

WHAT'S THE GOOD WORD?

Choose a student to read the Scripture for the day.

THE CHALLENGE

Go over each statement on the Fact or Opinion page, asking the students to tell you whether they thought each statement was a fact or an opinion. Say: **Jesus is Lord. That's a fact. Someone might disagree with it, but it's still true. Jesus is the Way. Jesus is the Truth. Jesus is the Life. Jesus is the Lord.** Tell the students that in their Discovery Centers today they will find out about God's plan to have all people recognize Jesus as Lord.

PRAYER

DISCOVERY CENTERS

Discovery Centers
Centers

1. "LORD OF ALL" CROSSWORD PUZZLE

DO: Give each student a copy of the crossword puzzle. Stand by to help them as needed while they work the puzzle.

> **MATERIALS**
> pencils, copies of the crossword puzzle on page 94, a Bible

DISCUSS: Ask someone to read the verse that they discovered by working the crossword puzzle. Ask: **How many things is Jesus greater than? How many things were made through his power?** Ask each student to name a foreign country that Jesus has authority over. Ask someone to read Genesis 12:1-3. Ask: **How many people on earth did God intend to bless through Abraham?** Say: **Even though God chose Abraham and eventually the nation of Israel to be his special people, from the very beginning, God wanted to bless all people. God wants Jesus to be Lord of all. Why?**

2. DETHRONED

MATERIALS
a Bible, construction paper, scissors, glue, permanent markers, magazines that would be appropriate for your students to look through (Note: You may have to tear inappropriate pages out of the magazines.)

DO: Give each student a piece of construction paper, a pair of scissors, and some glue. Instruct the students to look through the magazines and cut out pictures of things people might put first in their lives. These are things that might be more important to people than Jesus. Each student makes a collage of the pictures he cuts out by gluing them to the construction paper. Then tell the students to use a black magic marker and write across the top of the whole collage: DETHRONED.

DISCUSS: Ask someone to read John 12:31-32. Tell the students that Jesus said this when he was talking about his death. Ask: **What does this verse say that Jesus' death did?** (It drove out the ruler of this world.) **Who or what would that have been?** (Satan, evil, sin.) Say: **Jesus' death destroyed the power of sin in our lives. If we ask Jesus to be our Savior and Lord, we are free from the power of sin. Who is the ruler now?** Ask someone to read Matthew 28:18. Tell the students that this is what Jesus said after he had died and come back to life. Say: **God's plan is for everyone in the world to realize that Jesus is Lord. Someday everyone will bow before Jesus and admit that he is Lord.**

3. LORD ALL OVER THE WORLD

MATERIALS
copies of the world map (page 95), crayons or markers, a chalkboard or dry erase board, a Bible

DO: Give each student a copy of the world map. Write each of the following foreign words for "Lord" or "God" on the board, and tell students which language it is. They write the word on the map on the country in which that language is spoken. They can color in the map if you have time left.

Word—Where spoken
Bwana—Kenya, Africa
Raab—Jordan
Seigneur—France

Senor—Spain, Mexico

Kurie—Greece

Herr—Germany, Norway

Lord—England, USA, Canada, Australia

Dumnezeu—Romania

Zhu or Shoon—China

Boh—Belarusse

Pan—Czech Republic

Gud—Sweden

Ma'heo'o—Cheyenne Indian

DISCUSS: Ask someone to read Psalm 22:27. Ask: **What is it that God wants people to know about him?** Ask someone to read: Psalm 67:1, 2. Say: **This verse asks God to bless his people for a special reason. What is that reason?** Ask someone to read Psalm 86:9. Say: **God has his own idea of who he wants to see in a group worshiping him and praising Jesus. What would this group be like?** (There would be people from every nation, tribe, and language.)

DISCOVERERS' DEBRIEFING

If you have time to review, gather as a large group and discuss your young discoverers' findings. Ask the following questions:

- **What is the most interesting thing you discovered today?**
- **What did you learn today that you did not know before?**
- **How many people on earth did God intend to bless through Abraham?**
- **Why is Jesus the Lord of all?**
- **What did Jesus' death destroy?**
- **Who has all authority in heaven and earth now?**
- **Who will be in the group of worshipers that God wants?**
- **What does God want everyone in the world to confess?**

Review the Scripture for today.

Pray, thanking God for his great love for the whole world. Confess in prayer that Jesus is Lord.

Fact or Opinion?

Write **F** in the blank if the sentence is a Fact.
Write **O** in the blank if the sentence is an Opinion.

_____ Sugar is sweet.

_____ Sugar is delicious.

_____ Fire is hot.

_____ Fire is frightening.

_____ Cats are cute.

_____ Cats are animals.

_____ Rain is wet.

_____ Rain is exciting.

_____ Jesus is the Way.

_____ Jesus is the Truth.

_____ Jesus is the Life.

_____ Jesus is Lord of all.

Lord of All
Crossword Puzzle

Fill in the blanks below with the words you find in the crossword puzzle.

"[7] _____ [2] _____ has [4] _____ God, but Jesus is
[5] _____ [10] _____ him. [9] _____ ranks
[8 down] _____ than all the things that have been made. Through his
[3] _____ all things were made—things in [8 across] _____
and on [6] _____, things [4] _____ and [4]un_____,
all [3] _____s, authorities, [1] _____, and
[11] _____" (Colossians 1:15, 16, ICB).

Across

1. King of kings, Lord of _____
4. Ears have heard, eyes have _____
7. Opposite of yes
8. Opposite of hell
9. Another name for Jesus
10. The same as
11. People who rule

Down

2. What plus itself = 2?
3. Might, strength
5. Precisely, perfectly
6. The planet we live on
8. Opposite of lower

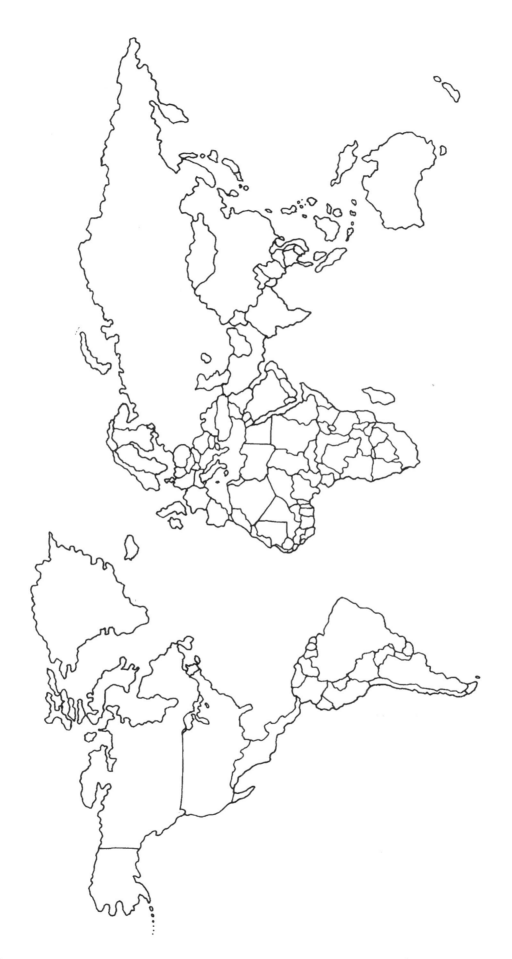

World Map